MEDICAL MISADVENTURES

To my teachers, both those who taught me in medical school and those who unwittingly became my teachers in later life.

CONTENTS

CONTENTS

PREFACE

*In a Hadith recorded by Muslim ibn al-Hajjaj, the
companion Abdullah, son of Masud, reported:
"The Prophet Muhammad said, 'There is not one
of you who does not have a jinni appointed to be
his constant companion.' They said, 'And you too,
O Messenger of Allah?' He said, 'Me too, but Allah
has helped me, and he has submitted, so that he
only helps me to do good.'"*

— *Islamic Hadith*
quoted from Tafseer Ibn Katheer

Welcome to *Medical Misadventures*, a collection of medical anecdotes and short stories distilled from my medical experiences,
spanning the time from medical school to retirement. Some of
these describe medical mishaps of various sorts, and some are
merely musings on medical issues of interest. These anecdotes do not illustrate the inspiring and ennobling moments
that highlight great medical careers. They are a collection of
the incidents that underscore our frailties as physicians; they
have taught me humour, humility, and perhaps some humanity.
Some are funny, some pathetic, and some are simply the unexpected results of encounters with unusual people.

All are based on real people and real events, though some
details have been changed to protect the innocent, or because
my memory has failed. In some stories names and places have
been disguised to avoid embarrassment to those who might
complain that the djinns[1] have treated them unfairly. That may
be so, but, in most cases, my recall suggests that the djinns have
been given ample opportunity.

My motivation for collecting these stories was simple. I
wrote them not to preserve them for posterity but to entertain

my friends. The only serious intent was to amuse, but if you find, *en passant*, a message in some of these anecdotes, I would be delighted. Some stories have footnotes with technical explanations for the enquiring reader. Like all medical writings, these are rather boring and can be skipped without much loss.

Recalling these anecdotes has again convinced me that I am saddled with a malevolent genie. Perhaps this is true for all physicians. My genie has infinite patience and a malign nature, and never leaves my back. He goes by many names: *impatience, haste, hubris, presumption, inattention,* and so on. He (and here I use the masculine deliberately) is always waiting to pounce, waiting for the moment I least expect him and when my defences are down. My only defence against him is constant vigilance. When my vigilance has faltered, the results have been occasionally amusing, often embarrassing, sometimes downright humiliating—and always with good reason for self-reflection. But, very occasionally, my djinn—like that of the Prophet Muhammad—was benevolent and did good. These moments represent the wonders of medicine, the magical events for which we have no explanation.

Because much of my career has been spent dealing with the problems of ill health, aging, and dying, these figure prominently in my stories. However, it is not my intent to be morbid, and I don't want morbidity to be the message in this volume. On the contrary! I am an optimist and upbeat about aging. Dying is part of living, and it is our mortality, at least the realization of our mortality, that gives meaning to life. This understanding is the catalyst for all human accomplishment. This idea, by the way, is not original to me (see Ernest Becker, *The Denial of Death*).[2]

I followed two criteria for selecting the anecdotes in this volume. First, each story is based on a real person or a real event, and each contains at least a nubbin of truth. Second, each is a once-in-a-lifetime experience. Those details that I want to emphasize as factual are identified by their sources. I hope my readers get as much enjoyment from reading these stories as I have had from writing them.

ACKNOWLEDGEMENTS

*To know even one life has breathed easier because you
    have lived,
This is to have succeeded.*

— *Ralph Waldo Emerson*

In writing these stories I owe more gratitude to more people than I can acknowledge in a few short paragraphs. The first command of the Hippocratic Oath is to honour your teachers. My teachers at the University of Manitoba Medical School and the Winnipeg teaching hospitals were exemplary role models. Joe Doupe, John Wade, Arnold Naimark, Brian Kirk, and many, many others guided my early steps in the medical world. I could not have asked for better teachers and mentors, and I express my gratitude for what they taught me—the basics of scientific medicine. Of course, I want to especially thank them for what was beyond their reach—what they couldn't teach me; otherwise there would be no book.

Patients and people with novel medical experiences have been the inspiration for the tales in this volume. Their stories have been enlightening and occasionally bemusing. The existential challenges have ended happily for some, but tragically for others. I have tried, in all cases, to treat their stories with consideration, sympathy, and respect.

My editors, Carol Dahlstrom and Patricia Sanders, have accomplished the huge task of converting my meanderings to readable prose. I owe them a huge debt of gratitude. Rachelle Painchaud-Nash has worked the manuscript into a beautifully designed book. Pam Simmons has been my mentor for promotions and publicity, things that doctors usually do ineptly. My wife, Glenyce, and my sons, Doug and Dean, have read my drafts and provided tremendous support and encouragement. Dean, a nationally acclaimed graphic artist when he was in the newspaper business, has provided the cover page and illustrations. Doug designed the logo for Bellefield Publishing.

I want to express particular appreciation to the readers of my blog, <www.arnoldtweed.com>, many of whom are old friends. Some have become regular correspondents: Michael Czuboka, Tom Coonan, Doug Craig, John Wade, Mike Lee, Mary Ann and Terry Dolan, Dave and Linda McDowell, Roz Dick, and more. Their thoughtful comments have been of inestimable value, and their encouragement much appreciated.

The rest is mine. I am responsible for any errors, omissions, or slights. For the most part, I have tried to avoid embarrassment, except to myself. Patient confidentiality has required me to falsify some names and places. However, the stories are all based on real events and real people, many of whom have consented to be identified by name.

MEDICAL MISADVENTURES

MISLEADING MOMENTS
AND CAUTIONARY CONFESSIONS

THE WRONG WIFE

Our most heroic efforts sometimes backfire. No medical drama on the streets is more galvanizing or more disorganized than is resuscitation from cardiac arrest. Crowds, hysterical relatives, and unfamiliar surroundings are distracting, and it is a tempting opportunity for my personal genie to take advantage of haste and confusion to play his tricks.

In the late summer of 1977, my young family and I were returning from Europe on Wardair, Max Ward's charter airline, which was eventually swallowed by Canadian Airlines. Since they had served good food and free booze on our transatlantic flight, I was in a mild state of foggy fatigue. We queued up for customs inspection at Winnipeg's international airport, shuffling our feet impatiently as the grim-faced customs officers methodically searched the suitcases of the pensioners in line ahead of us. The tremulous, perspiring old woman just in front of me should have caught my attention, but the August heat provided sufficient explanation for her perspiration and my mental lethargy.

Just as she heaved her suitcase onto the counter, she collapsed, folding up into a small, forlorn heap at my feet. That immediately ended my lethargy. Five years of teaching cardiopulmonary resuscitation (CPR) triggered the instinctive response: "Are you all right? Can you speak? Does anyone here know CPR? Call 911 for an ambulance." I followed the prescribed steps, opened the airway and   checked for breathing, but I knew she was in cardiac arrest. A crewcut young man, whom I later learned was a North Dakota state trooper, slid onto his knees beside me, and we started methodical two-man CPR: one-one-thousand, two-one-thousand . . . five-one-thousand—breathe. I swear that the customs inspector continued to examine the lady's suitcase as we sweated on the floor to save her life.

After what seemed like an eternity but was actually less than twenty minutes, a Winnipeg Ambulance Services crew arrived. In the zeal of the moment, I had no intention of leaving her fate in their hands alone, and we all piled into the ambulance—patient, state trooper, and me. Then, just as the crew was securing the stretcher, a small bald head timidly emerged at the ambulance door. His gaze drifted around the cabin as if searching for someone he knew, trying to make sense of this sudden tumult. "Is that my wife?" It was as much a statement as a question.

I had neither time nor patience to deal with this distraction. My response, "Does she look like your wife?" was answered hesitantly. "Yes, I think so," he said.

"Help him into the front seat, and let's get going."

In the ER, the emergency room, thirty minutes later, it was obvious she was not going to make it. Her cardiac arrest was unresponsive to bicarbonate, adrenaline, calcium, and several attempts at defibrillation. This was my hospital, my domain, my colleagues, and we were a smooth, functioning team. We had had many successful resuscitations from pre-hospital cardiac arrest, and we did our best, but this was not to be one of our saves. Reluctantly we stopped, and I went to find the small, bald, old man.

Informing the next of kin is never easy, but there is a standard formula that you follow, even when you're exhausted: find a quiet room, sit down, hold the hand of the bereaved, and break the news as gently as possible. "It was her heart, cardiac arrest," I said. "We tried our best, but we couldn't restart it. Yes, she has passed away. Yes, of course you can see her just as soon as the nurses tidy her up a bit."

I thought about my family, forgotten and marooned at the airport. For a minute I sat dejectedly at the nurses' desk, waiting for a chance at the telephone to call a cab. Anne, the charge nurse, was on the phone, listening but not talking. Then she cupped the phone in her hand and turned very slowly towards me. "Dr. Tweed," she said, "I hope I'm hearing this wrong. This call is from the security services at the airport. They've found a woman in a wheelchair—a large, loud, and very angry woman—and she's looking for her husband. And what she's threatening to do with him when she finds him should not be repeated by a nice girl like me. It seems they've also found a senile little old man who's lost his wife."

Let me digress for a moment. This story was told at a dinner party in Bahrain, twenty years later and half the circumference of the globe away. We were being hosted by Tom and Casey O'Leary, now living in Edmonton. I had known Tom as a resident; he had finished his anaesthesia training in Winnipeg a few years after I had. But the anecdote was really for the amusement of others, American friends who had been regaling us with tales of their own mishaps. Over the intervening years I had not repeated this story often, at least not until I thought that the principals were all dead and the story had been long forgotten by everyone but me.

"Yes," Tom said, "I remember that day. I was covering Emergency. Before I joined Anaesthesia, I worked as an ER doc. After you stopped the code and talked to the old man, I took him in to see his wife. He was bewildered and stroked her cheek, held her hand for a minute, then said he wanted to be alone with her."

The news from the airport had left me dumbfounded. I was dazed, and my first reaction was to hope it was a hoax. How can good intentions turn out so badly? You try to do what is right, what you've been trained to do, and the world conspires against you. My genie gloated: "Haste and impatience, Dr. Tweed. You assumed you controlled the situation; you were wrong!"

Meanwhile, Anne, ever resourceful, as ER head nurses must be, checked the identifications of the dead woman and the elderly man. The dead woman was definitely not his wife! Who would tell the old guy, and how could one explain such a fiasco?

I went back to the quiet room, held his hand, and spoke slowly, carefully choosing my words; this was not a task I had practised. "I'm sorry, Mr. Brown, for upsetting you so," I said, "but how could we know? The lady in the ambulance, yes, that lady in the other room, who is dead. Well, Mr. Brown, you see, we've made a terrible mistake. We don't think that lady is your wife, Mr. Brown. In fact, we're sure that she's not your wife. Your wife is at the airport. She's at the airport and she's looking for you."

He sat slumped over, hands folded, staring at the closed door, saying nothing. I didn't know if he had heard, or had understood, or was about to collapse himself. Then a tear slipped out of the corner of his eye and ran down his cheek. I left before I confounded my folly further.

A SNAKE GOT INTO THE ACT

One of the most memorable patients from my ICU (intensive care unit) days was an exotic dancer, a young woman who claimed to be of Mexican origin and had adopted "Juanita" as her stage name. Her partner, a young, virile western diamondback rattlesnake, played the straight man in her act.

Exotic dancers in Winnipeg were normally pub entertainers. In the main they were a pathetic lot. The only prop provided by the beverage-room owners was a small, elevated stage near the centre of the pub. In the larger pubs there would be three or four noon-hour acts. Each dancer would rush in, perspiring if it were summer and shivering if it were winter, clutching her meagre accessories. There was no introduction or any attempt at finesse. Each had to first set up her portable stereo player and select her music, then excite her audience.

Music blasting, she would begin her dance, provocatively exposing her body parts as she systematically removed her clothes and piled them in an untidy heap in a corner of the stage. Down to her G-string, she would gyrate her hips, more or less in synchrony with the music, make some suggestive thrusts at the front-row drinkers, dip her nipples in a couple of beer glasses, then grab her bundle of clothes and rush to dress in the women's toilet. A hasty exit was required, not to escape the clutches of the aroused audience but to be on time for the next engagement.

The men who frequented these pubs were a study in dissimulation. Though the front-row tables were always filled, those men lucky (or early) enough to claim those seats pretended that they were there only for the drinking. They studiously ignored the dancers, barely glanced at the stage, except when some part of the female anatomy was thrust into their field of vision. Otherwise they feigned total disinterest. No one could figure out what tempted them, or why the pubs with dancers thrived and those without failed.

But Juanita's act was different; for several months she was the most popular pub act in town. She teased her male audiences with her snake, which both captivated and repelled them. The snake has special sexual symbolism for some men; indeed, *trouser snake* is a vernacular term for the male organ. The snake evokes macho images of sexual strength and dominance: coiled but quick to lunge, dangerous, potent, and feared. Juanita capitalized on this male fascination with the reptile, and when she and her partner performed, they had the undivided attention of every man in the pub. Not a word was uttered, not a drop of beer drunk. The patrons, like the crowd at a tennis match, riveted their gaze on the snake's head as it disappeared between her thighs and craned their necks expectantly to see if it reappeared behind her. They didn't clap, of course, which would have suggested unbecoming interest. But they certainly didn't try to molest her either. Within a few weeks she had developed a certain notoriety among the good citizens, tempered, of course, with proper expressions of disapproval.

Apparently, the snake did not enjoy his role as much as was believed. One fateful day, near the climax of her act, he bit her. It is the natural thing for a western diamondback rattler to do when handled. Juanita was not naïve about snakes and had had his venom glands removed, but she had neglected to have him defanged. Since he was a robust young fellow, he left two very visible puncture marks. Perhaps he didn't have a full charge of venom on board, but we weren't about to take a chance. Juanita was admitted directly from emergency to the ICU, where we could provide the care and attention that her unusual condition deserved.

She was admitted to the ICU on a Thursday evening, and antivenin injections were begun that night. There was swelling and cyanosis around the puncture sites, but she adamantly refused to even consider surgical debridement, a standard treatment in those days. She argued that surgical disfiguration might make her unemployable. She had been bitten before and planned to go right back to work when we were finished with her.

By Friday morning every doctor in the hospital knew about our exotic patient and her mishap. Not only was snake envenomation a rare event in our subarctic climate, but the circumstances in which she had been bitten piqued the curiosity of our distinguished medical staff. Some may even have seen her act and knew how perilously close that snake's head came to her private (or not so private, in her case) parts. The medical teams came in droves, and every medical speciality made the ICU their first stop for rounds that day. Internal medicine, surgery, gynaecology, and every other hospital speciality (including sports medicine) dropped by. Her case obviously presented a unique learning opportunity for the students, interns, and residents and perhaps the case of the day for medical grand rounds.

Juanita was delighted to be the centre of attention. She welcomed her new admirers and was willing, even eager, to display her wounded part for their inspection. But, alas, their interest was short-lived. After a cursory glance, most decided they were late for more important tasks. Contrary to the rumour that had been started by a mischievous ICU resident, Juanita had not been bitten on her most tender parts. The snake had sunk his fangs into the web between her thumb and index finger, and the only part of her anatomy on public display was her right hand. Medical interest in her condition rapidly waned.

A DIAGNOSTIC TRIUMPH

Diagnostic acumen is the essence of the art of medicine and the hallmark of great physicians. It requires a mysterious combination of superior knowledge, extensive experience, and astute intuition. Some of these skills are acquired; some, innate. My first months as a junior intern had been insanely busy; my knowledge and intuition had been severely tested. In my modest self-assessment, I had not been found wanting! This anecdote describes a rare opportunity that was offered me to publicly demonstrate my newly honed diagnostic skills.

As a young intern at the City Hospital in the mid-1960s, before it became the Centre for Health Sciences, one of my first rotations was in the ER. Now, in 2018, the ER is a major department, staffed by specialists and equipped with X-ray and trauma rooms. But in 1965 it was just a couple of rooms with a few nurses and a doctor. For a junior intern it was the heart of the hospital, a theatre of daily drama and tragedy, and it was the service where interns became doctors. Before there were full-time emergency physicians, we junior interns staffed the ER in twelve-hour shifts. If we were desperate we might get a resident to come down from the wards and see a patient, but more often they were too busy and would send instructions to admit the patient directly to their service. There was a qualified surgeon nominally appointed as director, I think on a part-time basis, but he was rarely seen and I doubt I would have recognized him.

I saw 60 to 100 patients during each shift. Every day we managed cardiac arrests, trauma, and overdoses. All required an accurate diagnosis, sure judgment, and decisive action. Within just a few weeks I was confident that I could competently manage any medical emergency.

The incident that I describe occurred on a relatively tranquil evening in late summer. Thankful for a short respite, we were drinking coffee in the converted storeroom that served as a lounge. The phone call from some frightened parents that disturbed our peace was unusual but not enough to excite us. While changing the diaper of their two-year-old child, their first, the mother had noted a new appendage protruding from his anus. She had thoroughly inspected that orifice, and his other parts, each time she bathed him, and they had always before looked quite normal. They were bringing him in by ambulance.

Ten minutes later they arrived; both parents were frightened and upset, though the patient was remarkably unperturbed. The parents could add nothing to the brief history they had given by telephone. No problem there for an experienced ER doctor. All that was required was to undress the child, examine the offending appendage, and make the diagnosis. We all crowded into a small examining room: fidgeting patient, reassuring nurses, anxious parents, and me.

The parents' observations had been accurate: a small fecal-stained appendage, two or three millimetres in diameter and about two centimetres long, protruded from the child's anus. It didn't look like a diverticulum or a hemorrhoid, and I quickly narrowed the differential diagnosis with a few quick, astute questions. Had they noted any weight loss, rectal bleeding, or itching? Had they recently travelled in the tropics? Were there pets at home? Had they previously examined his stools? Although their responses to all questions were negative, it was obvious that we were dealing with some sort of intestinal parasite.

I had had the benefit of a traditional medical education with a well-organized set of lectures on helminthology, the study of parasitic worms, about three years earlier. My training in helminthology had also included lab sessions in which we examined formalin-preserved specimens of various tapeworms, roundworms, and pinworms in jam jars. This rote approach to medical education would dismay a modern educator, but I thought I had learned enough about the topic to cope with most problems encountered in a temperate zone. Admittedly, I hadn't viewed this as a high priority in my medical education and had attended the lectures with desultory interest. But I was confident I had enough basic knowledge of the subject to manage this simple problem competently. I had never actually seen an intestinal parasite outside a jar, and this specimen didn't resemble anything I could remember, but I was sure that a few simple investigative steps would serve to resolve the diagnosis satisfactorily.

The parents were reassured that this problem, though aesthetically unpleasant and perhaps requiring a little more attention to what went into his mouth, was not life threatening. I explained gently that intestinal worms were not indicative of bad parenting and that a simple antibiotic purge would cleanse the child's digestive tract. The next step was to don gloves and carefully extract the offending creature for more detailed analysis.

By this time we had attracted a small crowd. All the nurses not otherwise occupied had squeezed into our cramped cubicle to watch this delicate operation. I basked in the aura of an attentive and appreciative audience. The parents' level of anxiety decreased perceptibly, and they withdrew a little, perhaps overawed by the medical resources being mobilized to treat their child.

I pulled very carefully, steadily, and gently on the head (or tail) of the thing, and it yielded. One or two centimetres of the body slipped out, then a little more. All this was done with great delicacy and finesse since I wanted to extract the creature intact. There was total silence from my intent audience.

About thirty centimetres were retrieved in this fashion and coiled on a towel, but it kept coming. The diagnosis, which was becoming painfully obvious to me and had probably been apparent to the nurses all along, came to the parents in a flash of recall. The day before, they had seen the child playing with a long piece of white packing cord, sucking on one end, as two-year-olds will do. In their panic they had forgotten. Their change in attitude was palpable; they were suddenly much less impressed with my erudition.

The nurses drifted away to more interesting pursuits. Not one said a word or changed her expression of mild curiosity. I left the mother to extract the remainder of the string herself.

MUNCHAUSEN'S SYNDROME

Psychiatry was my last rotation as a junior intern. I had completed all the required rotations in medicine, surgery, pediatrics, and obstetrics, and considered myself, with justification, a savvy and battle-hardened young doctor, within a month of receiving my certificate to practise.

I had seen it all: pathos, mayhem and violence, and self-mutilation. I had witnessed nobility and courage in some patients and helpless defeat in others. I was ready for the world of medicine, not just the clinical challenges but also the challenge of reading patients—their needs, their fears, their intentions, and, above all, what they were hiding.

I expected that a month of psychiatry would be almost like ending my internship with a vacation. Since I was the only intern, I would be on call 24/7, but the caseload would be light and emergencies infrequent. Unlike with my previous services, a weekend on call promised to be a weekend of loafing at home.

The first call from the emergency room came about 10:00 p.m. on my first Friday. It was a common psychiatric problem: attempted suicide. The patient, Reginald R., had been brought to the ER by the police. Their story was simple and brief. The man in their custody had been standing on Portage Avenue at the bus stop in front of the Eaton Centre, chatting amicably with one of Winnipeg's finest, when he suddenly threw himself in front of an approaching bus.

The policeman, both quick-witted and nimble, pulled him back, but our patient fought him off and tried to scramble under the wheels of the bus, now stopped and loading late-night passengers. He ignored the advice freely offered by both the officer and the commuters—who only wanted to get home—and loudly declared his right to end his life.

Since he had to be physically extricated from under the bus, which was already behind schedule, the policeman was stuck with him. And, since it was also near the end of the officer's shift, he probably made a quality-of-life decision—quality of his own life, that is, certainly not mine. If he took Reggie to the ER of the City Hospital, he could turn him over to the constable on duty and go home; if he charged Reggie and locked him up, he would be stuck with two or three hours of paperwork.

Such were the life-or-death decisions that led to my summons to the ER at 10:00 p.m. on a Friday night to admit an attempted suicide. I wasn't particularly distressed; it was my only call of the evening, and attempted suicide was a legitimate admission. Once we got Reggie to the ward, it took a rather large dose of Valium to sedate him, but he soon went quietly to sleep, and I quickly followed suit.

I had the whole weekend to sort Reggie out, my first real psychiatric patient. Admittedly, I had some reservations that psychiatry was a real medical specialty, but I wanted to make a good impression in my last month, so I did a thorough medical examination as well as a psychiatric history. Reggie was a small, middle-aged man of no particular distinction. His manner was diffident, almost apologetic, his voice soft and pleading, and he paused after each statement as if judging its effect. He had the remarkable knack of watching you without staring. The only notable features of his physical examination were his abdominal scars, evidence of multiple surgical attempts to explore his innards, for reasons I could not immediately discover.

Reggie was more than willing to talk: he was downright eager. His was a story of tragedy and rejection. He told me about his abusive father, his thankless employer, his cheating wife, and his difficult childhood. He had been brought up in a poor family with a mother who did housecleaning, an older sister who went out every evening (he didn't know where) dressed mainly in mascara and hot pants, and a father who did odd jobs and drank. Most evenings his father would beat his mother until she surrendered her day's pay, and he beat Reggie, too, when he tried to defend her.

Reggie had left home at age sixteen after his mother died tragically, and he joined the army at the outbreak of World War II. During the war, he was a paratrooper, and he hinted that he had many harrowing experiences to relate—only, of course, if I were interested in listening. After demobilization he worked his way up from shipping clerk to dispatcher in a large trucking firm. Life was going well until he developed serious medical problems. He had no medical or disability insurance, but his doctor insisted he have a laparotomy (surgical intra-abdominal exploration) to diagnose his pain. After the operation he was worse, and his misery was compounded; he had no job, no savings, no severance pay, no benefits.

That was when he discovered that his wife was cheating on him with his best friend. One afternoon, exhausted from his fruitless search for work—"any job," as he put it—he came home early and found his wife and friend in bed together. She was unapologetic, berating Reggie for being sick and out of work. He left and tried to get himself straightened out but struggled with depression. He had found very few people who were willing to help him, and medical people had proven particularly disappointing.

He had been diagnosed, he informed me, with gastric epilepsy, and the conspicuous scars on his abdomen were evidence of many fruitless surgical attempts to relieve his agony. When the attacks came the pain was excruciating, tempered only by large doses of Demerol. But some doctors—and here he became bitter and resentful—rejected him, just as his wife had done. They treated his attacks with placebos—that is, injections of normal saline. He could tell the difference between placebos and the real thing immediately and could hardly believe that trained doctors and nurses, who had taken the Hippocratic Oath, would let another human suffer as he suffered. He hoped that I was not of that ilk.

A half-hour after I had left the ward, I had a call from the charge nurse. Reggie was having one of his seizures, clutching his abdomen in agony, crying for help. I immediately went back to examine him and found him, as described, writhing with pain. "Unbearable," he moaned. When I examined his abdomen, he complained of excruciating tenderness wherever I probed, but he didn't have the rigidity, guarding, and lack of bowel sounds typical of an acute abdominal crisis.

He pleaded that I not leave him in agonizing pain for the whole night as others had done. My first inclination was to get a second opinion, a surgical consult, but the surgical residents were busy exploring a knife wound and then had a perforated appendix to deal with before they could even consider my patient. I gave Reggie intravenous Demerol, and only after a remarkably large dose did he relax and, with a satisfied smile, fall asleep. There were two more such episodes between then and Monday morning, but adequate doses of Valium and Demerol ensured that both of us got some sleep.

On Monday morning rounds I presented Reggie to my staff psychiatrist. He was a hardened veteran of many encounters with the inner-city residents, and, after my detailed presentation, it took him less than fifteen minutes to assess Mr. Reginald R. His instructions were terse: "Discharge him with no medications." I was amazed at his penetrating perception, but he had some information he neglected to share with me. The previous week, before I had joined the service, a city-wide psychiatric conference had discussed a case with many of the features exhibited by Reggie. Perhaps it was the same person. The case was labelled *Munchausen's syndrome*, and all psychiatrists were cautioned to be wary.

I went back, rather chagrined, to break the bad news to Reggie. He had already packed his meagre belongings and left. He saw it coming, and probably not for the first time!

Munchausen's syndrome is one of the oddities of human nature, and its etymology has colourful origins. The first and still the best medical description of the condition was offered by a British physician, Dr. Richard Asher. In an article published in *The Lancet* in 1951, he described how, "like the famous Baron von Munchausen, the persons affected have always travelled widely;

and their stories, like those attributed to him, are both dramatic and untruthful. Accordingly, the syndrome is respectfully dedicated to the baron, and named after him."[1] The official label now is *factitious disorders,* a rather bland descriptor, and I prefer the old term.

The famous Baron Munchausen was a fictional character invented by an eighteenth-century German author, Rudolph Erich Raspe. In Raspe's accounts the baron is a braggart soldier who entertains his friends with implausible stories. But legend holds that he was a real person, a German aristocrat who served with the Russians during the Russo-Austro-Turkish War of 1735 and later became a raconteur of some notoriety. His stories are still remembered in parts of Europe.

Munchausen's syndrome patients are ingenious in concocting factitious symptoms. They baffle their caretakers in numerous ways: for example, by contaminating lab tests (putting sugar in urine samples is a common ploy), injecting fecal material into the skin to produce abscesses, inserting foreign bodies into various body orifices (including the urethra), ingesting drugs or chemicals, and much more.

The syndrome is not widely reported in the medical literature; it does not excite young doctors who are trying to bolster their academic credentials. The largest review—455 cases—was compiled in 2016 by G. P. Yates and M. D. Feldman from King's College, London.[2] They found that about two-thirds of reported cases were females (average age of thirty-four years), many with a psychiatric history. Unfortunately, most reports are simply descriptive, and there is little insight into the patients' bizarre behaviour.

Munchausen's syndrome is a perplexing mental disorder characterized by a craving for medical treatment, even surgery. Patients will go to great lengths to satisfy that craving, as the scars on Reggie's abdomen proved.

Munchausen's can be confused with a condition called *malingering,* but malingering stems from a different motivation. Malingerers feign illness for material gain: for example, to avoid work or military service. Munchausen's and malingering are both different from *hypochondria*. A hypochondriac truly believes that she—and most are women—has a serious or even fatal disease, and no amount of reassurance or negative tests will convince her otherwise.

To make matters even more complicated, there is also a *Munchausen-by-proxy syndrome*, in which the symptoms are feigned or induced in a child, often by the child's mother. This gets medical attention since the victims are young and vulnerable and likely to become adults with Munchausen's.

But most doctors and nurses have little sympathy for adult Munchausen's patients. They are viewed as malingerers, and their caregivers are offended by their deceptive and manipulative behaviour. There is no charitable foundation canvassing on their behalf, no trust to fund research into the cause.

No effective treatment has been reported for Munchausen's, and, in any case, patients with this syndrome show no interest in being cured. They are elusive, adept at deceiving young doctors and nurses, and vanish as soon as their deceptions are revealed. They are the phantoms that haunt emergency rooms, lurking in the shadows at the fringes of society and disappearing as soon as the light is shone on them.

Reggie, like the Baron Munchausen of old, was an entertainer, an itinerant storyteller, who played to a credulous audience of one. His reward was a whole weekend in which his cravings were indulged.

A MOST DISCREET PATIENT

T he rogues of this story wouldn't be recognized as such today. Both are successful and well-respected medical specialists, exemplary role models for the residents and interns entrusted to their teaching. One has just received a distinguished alumnus award from our alma mater. At the time of the incident I recall here, however, they were hell-raisers, their pranks familiar to a generation of staff and trainees at the City Hospital. If there were mischief afoot, one or both were sure to be behind it. The incident described in this story is exceptional because, for obvious reasons, it was not publicized. It was a scam concocted while both were junior residents in the ICU. I think that only two other people, a patient and myself, knew the full story.

The patient, Mr. S., had been admitted to intensive care, ward H7, for treatment of an intractable cardiac arrhythmia. Despite exposure to all the usual anti-arrhythmic drugs, and some that were still experimental, he continued to generate an alarming number of ectopic ventricular beats. Since he was not incapacitated by his condition, it was unnecessary to confine him to bed. Also, we wanted to see how exercise affected his heart condition. Fitted with a Holter monitor that he could slip into a pocket of his bathrobe, he had the complete freedom of the ICU. We were nervous about his going farther in case he had a bout of malignant arrhythmia, but within these confines, Mr. S. was our guest for several weeks. His only medical problems were the occasional side effects of his treatments, but his heart otherwise ignored every medication proffered. His perambulations around the ICU became part of our daily routine.

Mr. S. and I became friends. At that time I was the senior resident in the ICU, but he was a cardiology patient and not my direct concern. Most days we would have a brief chat over a cup of coffee. He was quiet and introspective, kept his own counsel, and patiently endured his doctor's experimentation. When he wasn't walking, he read. His habits were monkish; he was certainly not one given to vices or excesses. He was a good-natured, private, thoughtful chap.

When Mr. S. began to look like a permanent fixture, I suggested to my two junior residents that it was time to talk with his attending cardiologist about freeing up his bed. They would not hear of it. He might have a fatal arrhythmia, they argued. The consulting cardiologist was sure that a new drug would work, but it had to be closely monitored for a few days. His arrhythmia was of a rare type and was invaluable to their cardiology education. Since they rarely went near him, I thought their intense interest in his condition rather odd, but I accepted their protestations.

Not long after that, Mr. S. decided to confide in me. He approached me discreetly one afternoon when the residents were out of the unit. We were standing in front of the director's office, where the inbox for mail and pharmacy supplies was located. Speaking in a quiet voice, with a hand on my arm, he indicated his concern only by the intensity of his manner.

"Dr. Tweed," he said, "I must have a word with you. This has been bothering me for some time now, and I think you should be informed. You know that I walk up and down this hallway several times every day. I mind my own business and I don't talk much, but I keep my eyes open and I don't miss much either. Now, every day I glance into this box to see if there are any cards for me. Every day there is a box from the pharmacy here, containing six bottles of beer, with my name on it. Dr. Tweed, I haven't touched alcohol in years, and this is a puzzle to me."

I doubt that it was much of a puzzle to Mr. S., and it certainly wasn't to me. Beer was available from the pharmacy, by prescription, as an appetite stimulant or general comforter for some patients. Mr. S. was the only patient on the ward taking a regular diet, ergo the only one for whom a daily beer prescription would not raise questions. It wasn't difficult to guess who might be quaffing his beer. A short walk up the back stairs to the residents' call room confirmed my suspicion. One wall was almost hidden by a stack of beer cases, filled with empty bottles. And my two self-indulgent junior residents were happily settled in front of the television, each fondling a bottle of Labatt.

They were neither chagrined nor apologetic, but I was reluctant to start an investigation that would probably get them dismissed from the hospital. Despite their bad behaviour, they were good doctors. However, continued misappropriation of the hospital's supplies would certainly land us all in trouble. So we reached a compromise. Mr. S. would be discharged, the empty beer cases would disappear, and I would develop temporary amnesia. Pharmacy prescriptions in the future would be reserved for patients only.

I was confident that Mr. S. would keep his own counsel, and I was right. He was a most discreet patient, and, having done his duty, he said nothing more about the affair.

A VISIT TO THE DOCTOR

When I was a young doctor, just past internship, I supplemented my income by doing locums in rural areas, filling in for the local doctor. A *locum* is a temporary fixture, not part of the community, and consequently not acquainted with its customs. For a city boy, this could be a daunting experience; country folk tended, at least in those days, to describe their health and medical problems in a manner intended to leave the listener baffled. Fortunately, I was born and raised in rural Manitoba, and the discourse of country people was second nature to me. The key was to understand their main obsession, which was to give nothing away. Only essential information was revealed, and that grudgingly. The doctor, or anyone else listening, heard only what they wanted him to hear.

The location of this story is of no importance; it could have been anywhere west of Winkler to the Saskatchewan border. My first patient on my first morning was Mr. J., age fifty, a farmer. The file handed me by the receptionist was blank; this was his first clinic visit. He entered the examining room hesitantly, politely removed his John Deere cap, and waited until I motioned him to a chair. A farmer and his cap were seldom separated, except for two events, probably viewed with equal distaste: funerals and visits to the doctor.

I believe in the adage that first impressions count, so I prepared carefully for locums—newly starched lab coat, name tag, white shirt and tie, fresh haircut. My patient was also dressed for the occasion (probably by his wife) in not-quite-funerary garb but better-than-usual, going-to-town garb: clean shirt, dress shoes, and new cap. From my vantage point behind the desk, I could sense that he was uncomfortable. Something here was not as he had expected. His gaze shifted quickly about the room, as if he were looking for an escape route.

But time was pressing, and there were already a dozen patients in the waiting room. I started briskly. "Good morning, Mr. J. I'm Dr. Tweed, and it seems this is your first visit to this clinic."

"I guess so. Where is the old doc, Dr. Woods?"

I explained to him that Dr. Woods was attending a refresher course and then taking a vacation, and I was his substitute for two weeks. This established, I was eager to get down to business. With a new patient it is generally useful to get some information about past medical problems, so I like to start with a brief medical and surgical history.

"Right, Mr. J. Have you ever been sick in the past or had any surgical operations?"

"Yeah, once in a while."

"And what sort of sickness have you had?"

"Oh, the usual things."

"And operations?"

"No."

"Now, by 'the usual things,' what exactly do you mean?"

Hesitation. "Oh, the sort of things a kid gets."

"You mean you've had the usual childhood diseases: mumps, measles, chicken pox?"

"Yeah, I guess so."

"Right, Mr. J., and what brought you here this morning?"

"Oh, my wife drove me."

"Well, yes, Mr. J., I'm happy to hear that. What I really meant was, what did you want to talk to me about?"

"Ah! I came in to ask you about a little problem I have."

"Oh, and could you describe this problem?"

"Yeah! I guess I could." There followed a long pause, during which he gazed at the ceiling as if seeking divine inspiration.

I grew impatient. "Yes, and if you were to describe it, what would you say?"

"Well, I'm not feeling very good."

"Not feeling good, and how long have you not been feeling good?"

"Oh, quite some time."

"Would you say days, weeks, months?"

"Yeah, something like that."

We were now about five minutes into the medical history, on a busy clinic day, and I had learned almost nothing about Mr. J. or why he had come in. Either he was especially obtuse or remarkably stupid, or he was hiding something. Perhaps he had a medical issue or concern that he was afraid to mention, something he hoped I would guess without his having to find the words. Or perhaps he was testing me. It was a notion held by some country folk in those days that, if the doctor was so smart, especially a young doctor, he would be able to figure out what was wrong with you; you shouldn't have to tell him. I decided that it was time for the more tedious but reliable method of getting a history: direct questioning.

"Now, Mr. J., I am going to ask you some specific questions about your current health. I just want you to answer yes or no. First, do you have any pain?"

"No, not right now."

"Was it because of a pain that you came to see me this morning?"

"No."

"Was it because of a sexual problem?"

"No."

The list could be long and would continue until I got a yes.

"Is it because you are feeling weak or tired?"

"Yeah. That's it. I can hardly walk to the barn before I get tired."

We were now about ten minutes into the medical history and only starting to make progress. His chief complaint, with which we usually begin a medical history, was fatigue. In a fifty-year-old man, there could be many reasons for fatigue, but at this pace further history taking was a poor investment of my time. The next step was a physical examination and some basic lab tests. The physical examination showed nothing abnormal, the lab tests were scheduled, and I advised him to come back in a week.

The next week he was a little more talkative, either because he had tested me enough or because he was more worried.

"Good morning, Mr. J. How are you today?"

"Oh, about the same."

"Are you still feeling tired when you walk to the barn?"

"Yeah."

He looked hopeful, but my news was not good. His laboratory tests were unremarkable, except for one. He was seriously anemic; his hemoglobin level was much below normal. Fatigue and anemia in a man his age were probably due to chronic internal blood loss. The most likely site was the large bowel.

"Mr. J., I have to do a rectal examination. That means I put a finger in your rectum to feel around. But first, tell me, has there been any problem with your bowel movements?"

His head jerked upward as if I'd snapped my fingers. Now there was no gazing at the ceiling for inspiration or vague dissembling; something about his bowels worried him, and I had somehow guessed it.

"Yeah, I've had some black-looking shit in the last couple of months. Does that mean anything serious?"

It was a reasonable question. His black shit had worried him, but he had meant to keep it a private matter, not something to talk about and not with a new doctor. The reason he had come last week, or had been forced by his wife to come, was that he was feeling tired, not because of black shit.[1] He hadn't really associated the two.

The rectal examination did not reveal a tumour within reach of my index finger, but his stool was black, and the guaiac test (the test for occult blood) was positive.[2] The bleeding came from his large bowel; it was likely a tumour, but whether it was benign or malignant could not be determined at this stage. What he needed next was a surgical consultation, a biopsy, and probably a bowel resection. I had done all that I could do.

Once all the cards were on the table and the bad news was out, Mr. J. was a different man. He seemed relieved and wanted to move ahead. There were a lot of questions, a lot of decisions.

Harvest was coming up; but how would he manage if he were sick? Should he keep his son home from college? (I wondered silently how an eighteen-year-old who was looking forward to the freedom of college life would respond to the offer to spend another year or two on the farm.) What should he tell his wife? If he delayed the operation until winter, would he recover in time for spring seeding? Seeding and harvesting were the mile-stones in a farmer's year; everything revolved about them. All other issues, including health, were secondary.

Of course, I had no answers to these questions, but discussing them was his priority and probably restored some sense of control in his life. We parted on amicable terms, and I never saw him again.

Mr. J.'s surprising openness at the end of his second visit was a striking contrast to his taciturn responses earlier. Why are some people so vague, and why do they find it so difficult to discuss their medical problems? Perhaps they simply lack the vocabulary, just as some lack a vocabulary for sexual discussions —except for the one universal descriptor, of course. Perhaps they fear the answer or are testing their doctor, or perhaps they simply don't understand the script their doctor is trying to follow.

At that time I believed that vagueness was a protective mechanism, part of the natural reticence of country people. In a small, gossipy community, personal affairs are carefully guarded. People don't air their private business in public, no matter how long they have known their neighbours. And they don't discuss their personal habits with a stranger, even a doc-tor, and certainly not a smart-ass young doctor just out of med-ical school.

Much later in my career, I came to appreciate another dynamic for this type of patient encounter—the dissonance in dialogue between patient and doctor. Using the theatre as an analogy and the patient visit as an act in a play, I—a newly minted and enthusiastic young doctor—saw myself as both the director of the performance and the main character. I thought I controlled the plot, the dialogue, and the outcome. But in medicine this type of thinking is pure fantasy! In fact, we are merely characters in others' plays, plays whose plots we can only guess. We do not direct; we merely play our parts and speak our lines.

The duality of the doctor's role is neatly illustrated in a recent article in the humanities section of the *Canadian Medical Association Journal* entitled "Parentheses," written by S. Arya, a Japanese-Canadian medical resident in the University of Toronto program. In the article she describes her medical residency as a series of scripted encounters with patients in which she, in the role of doctor, performs a set of task-oriented actions. But these are punctuated by interludes when she is just an empathetic listener. During the interludes she hears the personal narrative of the patient, and that is when she gets to know her patients, "by their existence as humans, with limitations and desires and fear and hope."[3] In our medical dramas, the real needs of our patients are heard during the intermissions, when the doctor becomes just another character, not the director.

MEMORABLE CHARACTERS,
AND A DOG

IN MEMORY OF GARM

In Norse mythology Garm is the ferocious hound who guards the gates of hell. Our Garm bore little resemblance to his mythical namesake. Guard dog he was not; he treated open gates as pathways to adventure, not to be guarded. In this incarnation Garm was strictly a family pet, or, more precisely, our boys' pet. When we adopted him, they were fourteen and nine years old; he was three months. Garm was a black Labrador retriever, or mostly so, and, true to his breed, was gentle, friendly, and handsome. Most of the time he was quite likeable and might even be credited with some intelligence, though his later behaviour would cast doubt on that assumption. In particular, he had the one quality that distinguishes all Labs: a good nose. This product of genetic selection, over which he had no control, was eventually to be the cause of his downfall.

Garm was a house dog but with limited privileges. The house rules were simple but strict; he had a pad in the kitchen and was to stay there. However, like the camel in *Arabian Nights*, he was always prepared to test the limits. While we were eating dinner, Garm would lie just in the doorway between kitchen and dining room with his nose exactly at the dividing line between the two. First the tip of his snout would edge across the border, followed by half his head and one paw very gingerly, then very slowly and quietly the other would follow. All this without a sound, trying his very best to be invisible. "Out, Garm," not even spoken harshly, and he would recoil back to his lair in the kitchen. He never required or received physical punishment; harsh words were quite enough to make him obey, if only temporarily.

When he was alone with the boys, he knew he had the freedom of the house. Of an evening, he would snuggle between them, relaxing comfortably on a soft chesterfield in the upstairs family room, watching TV or dozing. But the moment a car entered the driveway, signalling the return of parents, he bolted back to his place in the kitchen. Usually, he beat us and would raise his head sleepily as we entered the house, as if asking what had kept us so late. Occasionally, perhaps because the TV was too loud or the sitcom too engrossing or he was sleeping too soundly, he missed the noise of car tires crunching gravel and didn't realize his peril until the front door opened. Then he came careening down the stairs, tumbling head over heels in his haste, with no pretence at deception, to cringe under his blanket in the kitchen.

He was the boys' pet, and you can probably guess the division of responsibilities for his care. I fed him; they treated him to snacks. I took him out each day, summer and winter, for his E & E (exercise and excretion); they encouraged him to loaf with them in the family room. I disciplined him; they indulged him. Did this indulgence foster the character flaws that later led to his problems with the law? I suspected so, but I got little support for that view, neither then nor now.

We were a reasonably peaceful household until Garm started to feel the surges of young manhood. I realized that his brain was subservient to his hormones when he picked a fight with the neighbours' German shepherd, four times his weight and strength. My intervention certainly saved his life and cost me several lacerations and a tetanus shot. Garm was unabashed and acted as if he had won the fight. At that point I should have done the obvious and removed the source of his surging hormones. I procrastinated, and events overtook us.

As I said, Labs have good noses. Garm could sense the pheromones of a bitch in heat from across the city. He started to bolt from the yard, completely ignoring our calls to stop, and several hours later we would find him with a pack of similar-minded juvenile louts, vying for the attentions of a preening female. When we dragged him home, he seemed contrite but did not reform his behaviour. The next enticing waft of a bitch in estrus and he was off again.

Garm was confined to quarters. I reinforced the fence around our yard, two metres high with sharpened pickets along the top. The gate was kept locked, and when outside the yard he was always on a leash. Still I avoided the obvious solution.

Then disaster struck: the nadir of his delinquent career. Garm was a little short of his second birthday. It occurred on a late afternoon in mid-winter; we were all indoors, preoccupied by routine tasks. Garm was more alert than was his usual habit at that time of the day, but he studiously avoided the door, avoided even glancing at it. Interested in going outside? Not him! The front doorbell rang, and I forget now who the caller was or what his purpose. The door opened briefly, only a little, and Garm was gone. Like a sprinter out of the starting blocks, a black projectile, he bolted past the surprised caller, bounded to the top of a small snow pile bordering the walkway, and launched himself at the closed gate. Unfortunately for him, he cleared it with room to spare and disappeared. A search until dark of his usual haunts proved fruitless. The boys were inconsolable.

Two days later the city's poundkeeper phoned. Garm had been apprehended, and his offence was serious: caught with a pack of dogs in Assiniboine Park, chasing deer. The only one with a collar, he was positively identified. The boys were delighted; they wanted him home at once. The fine to spring him was fifty-three dollars and would increase for every day he was an unclaimed guest of the City. I was at work; grocery money on hand was insufficient; piggy banks were emptied, and there was still not enough. My wife claims that she had to search behind the cushions for loose change. I didn't witness Garm's release, but apparently he was a sorry specimen: fawning, contrite, and apologetic. How could a decent young fellow have sunk so low? Oh, the evils of bad company!

I was resolved that the definitive treatment could not be further delayed. The source of his tempestuous hormone surges had to be removed. It had been a busy day at the hospital and we had guests coming for dinner, but the poundkeeper had warned us that the fine would double each time he was caught. My research lab was quiet, so the chief lab technician was alerted and Garm was bundled off to our animal operating room.

My experience with veterinary anaesthesia had been limited to one species: sheep. Our sheep were docile, phlegmatic creatures that readily accepted a mask with halothane and oxygen. Compared with a sheep's breath, it was a fragrant mixture, and that might explain their lack of resistance. We usually induced general anaesthesia with about 3 per cent inspired halothane. Using an old ether bottle opened about halfway, we could expect to deliver anywhere from 2 to 5 per cent. However, we had done this at least a hundred times and had never killed a sheep.

Garm was contrite but, suspecting he was to be punished, he cowered; he whined; he cringed under the bench; he struggled when offered the mask with sweet-smelling halothane. His adrenaline level soared. I sat on him and opened the old ether bottle a little more, trying to get through this trauma quickly. In my impatience I forgot, or perhaps I never knew, some basic dog physiology. Dogs have an irritable myocardium and are prone to adrenaline-induced arrhythmia.

My readers will by now have guessed the sad ending to this story. Every anaesthetist knows the risks of mixing high levels of endogenous adrenaline, an irritable heart, and halothane anaesthesia. Garm struggled a little, then suddenly became quite still; the knife never got near his tender parts. When I saw his dilating pupils, I instantly realized what had happened: cardiac arrest. We tried to resuscitate him but to no avail. I considered calling 911 for a defibrillator, but Wayne, my technician, balked. He was, perhaps, anticipating tomorrow's headline in the *Winnipeg Free Press*: "Laboratory Technician Wayne P. at CSH Calls Paramedics to Resuscitate Mongrel Dog."

Although I could justify the necessity for my actions, the outcome was certainly a product of haste and carelessness. I could anticipate the questions and reproach that faced me at home. After all, Garm had left home a lively and healthy dog for a small operation that would cure him of his lusts. Would they think I had killed him deliberately? Would they doubt my sincerity and good intentions? I was a professional anaesthetist; would this blunder stigmatize my career? My genie gloated.

There were tears, of course, and reproach, and a heaping dollop of guilt and remorse. How did I explain my miscalculation? I fell back on the anaesthetist's oldest and lamest excuse: he took the anaesthetic badly. It was a low point for us all.

Why do dogs have such an emotional hold on us? First, consider that the domestic dog (*Canis familiaris*) and humans have a long shared history: 20,000 to 30,000 years.[1] Still, it is debatable who adopted whom; did wolves attach themselves to hunter-gatherer groups to share in the spoils of the hunt, or did humans capture and domesticate the now-extinct, megafaunal wolf? Though they may have hunted together, they were not chummy; that came much later. When hunting strategies became more dependent on dogs, the relationship deepened. Dogs were even buried with humans as trusted servants of the deceased. After the shift to an agricultural economy, about 12,000 years ago, dogs took on more domestic roles as herders, pack animals, and guard dogs, and we have lived more closely since. Domesticated dogs have thus had about 12,000 years to study humans, learn their body language, and anticipate their moves. They do this so well that we have anthropomorphized them; we assume their behaviour reflects human feelings and qualities. It is understandable that people put their dogs in their wills, delay vacations when their dogs are ill, and are prepared to pay their veterinarians more than they pay their doctors. Dog owners assume that the unconditional loyalty and love of their pet deserves a reciprocal response.

But dogs, some more than others, carry traces of the wolf ancestor. That is what shapes my memories of Garm. He was a dog that, at his best, was totally civilized: obedient, charming, and lovable. But when the instincts of the wolf were stirred, he acted like a wolf. He followed his nose and did what nature demanded of him.

The boys have a different point of view. They favour the old myths that portray dogs in mystical and heroic settings. Mythology is well populated with dogs: Garm in Norse mythology,

Cerberus in Greek, the wolf in Roman legend who suckled Romulus and Remus. Constellations and stars honour dogs. Sirius, the Dog Star in the constellation Orion, is the brightest star in the heavens. These are the images they relish. They see Garm, the black hound of Hel and guardian of Gnipa's Cave, leading a pack of savage wolves across the heavens into the battle of Ragnarok.

Fight bravely, Garm! Your reward is waiting in Assiniboine Park.

MARY B.

Canada's Indigenous peoples are much maligned. Doctors see them at both their worst and their best. At their worst, in the ER, we see them bruised and bleeding, victims of the mayhem and violence that stem from alcohol abuse. At their best, we see the stoicism, resilience, humanity, and humour that shape their inner character, even in the face of adversity.

Inevitably, we base our judgments on very brief encounters and seldom realize that, while we are pinning labels on them, they are doing the same to us. This is probably subtler when the interaction is unequal, when the white person is in a dominant role. In doctor–patient relationships, the doctor always plays the dominant role and patients, especially if they are Indigenous, are passive. Their satisfaction (or dissatisfaction) may surface on social media or personal blogs but, when this story unfolded, they generally remained silent.

Our First Nations people are particularly inscrutable, and they rarely reveal their inner thoughts, especially to whites. A long history of mistrust has made them cautious. Mary B., perhaps inadvertently, let that mask of inscrutability slip for a moment. In that moment she revealed a level of insight that left me both amazed and chagrined. This is her story.

One summer, when I was a young crusading doctor, I did a locum in The Pas, Manitoba, then a small pulp-and-paper town on the banks of the Saskatchewan River. It has achieved some notoriety recently because of an old unsolved murder. It seems that everyone in town, except the police, knew the three white boys who had raped and murdered an Indigenous girl fifteen years previously. That murder is not part of this story but was one episode in a history of mistreatment that nurtured long roots of mistrust and anger between the two communities.

Many whites abused Indigenous people; some tried to reform them. Both attempts were sources of resentment, which was usually well concealed.

In order to appreciate the events of Mary B.'s mishap, you have to know the peculiar geography of The Pas. The townsite was located on the south side of the river, directly across from the Opaskwayak Reserve, where most of the Indigenous people lived. There were two bridges across the river: a railway bridge and a road bridge. The Canadian National Railway line (now the Hudson Bay Railway) bisected the town, spanned the river with a long steel bridge and one set of rails, and continued through the reserve to Churchill. Each week, at 2:00 a.m. every Sunday, the Churchill Express roared through the town and over the bridge. Stern warnings posted at both ends of the bridge cautioned pedestrians not to use it as a shortcut to town.

The road bridge, which provided the only pedestrian walkway across the river, required people of the reserve to take a detour of about a kilometre south and the same back to get to the town.

Mary was a good citizen who worked during the week to support her family of three school-aged children. I never saw or heard her mention a male provider. She came regularly to the health clinic for treatment of her diabetes and chronic cough. When I examined her she was quiet, respectful, almost taciturn, and didn't waste our time with idle chatter. Her main concern seemed to be to get back to her work and family. Mary had some vices, minor or major, depending upon your moralistic bent. She was too fond of sweets and cigarettes, and it was therefore frustrating to treat her diabetes and bronchitis. I tried to educate her, and she listened politely, but my lectures had absolutely no effect. Her other vice, and apparently her sole source of recreation, was to get drunk on Saturday nights, a ritual practised in most small towns in western Canada. Mary's habits were not exceptional; most of her contemporaries did the same, as did most of the whites.

Generally, Mary and a small entourage of fellow revellers would walk into town after supper on Saturday evenings.

Because it was still daylight in summer and they were sober, law-abiding citizens at that time of the evening, they would make the long trek using the highway to the road bridge. It was well known that after the pub closed, most would return by using the shortcut across the railway bridge.

Mary and her company would go directly to the Paskoyac Lounge and Beverage Room. By the time the bar closed at midnight, they would all be quite soused, some staggering drunk, and some belligerent.

I was on duty in the ER that weekend, but it had been quiet, with only one or two minor cases. About 3:00 a.m. the telephone ended my slumber. As always, I was awake before the first ring ended, preparing mentally for the summons to patch up wounded antagonists from the inevitable late-night brawls. The ER charge nurse was apologetic. "Don't rush," she said. "It's only Mary B. Her drunken friends found her on the railway bridge about a half-hour ago, after the train went through. She made it about halfway across. She must have passed out and was run over. You'll have to pronounce her and sign the death certificate before we can send her to the morgue, but take your time. We'll cover the body with a sheet and keep it in the ER until you can come."

I arrived about fifteen minutes later to officiate at what appeared to be a tragic but routine ceremony. Removal of the sheet and a cursory examination revealed that she was indeed dead—dead drunk. Painful stimuli elicited a grunt but no eye opening. The only remarkable physical findings were the stench of booze and complete absence of any signs of recent trauma. There were no lacerations or bruises that were not several days old, and absolutely no sign of head injury. Since she was breathing and otherwise stable, I decided to put her in the recovery position and let her sleep it off.

Next morning, Mary was awake, sitting up in bed, her head cradled in her hands. She was suffering from that remorseless tyrant of the once-a-week drinker: an awful hangover. As well, she was confused about why she wasn't home in her own bed. Although she remembered part of the evening, she couldn't recall leaving the pub or starting across the railway bridge. I explained the events, as best we knew, that had brought her to us. She had left the pub shortly after midnight and had fallen asleep, or had passed out, on the railway bridge. Fortunately for her, she must have stretched out between the rails. The Churchill Express roared over her on its regular run, without even touching her or wakening her. When her friends found her, they thought she was dead and had brought her to the hospital.

Mary listened to this account in complete silence; her way was not to interrupt or question the word of authority. She was attentive, pensive, perhaps contemplating her near miss and good fortune to be alive. Maybe this was to be the turning point in her life, cleansing her of her vice and bad habits. Would she see the hand of God in her salvation? A chance to redeem herself? Although certainly not an evangelist, I saw this as an opportunity for some explicit health education in the guise of a moral lesson. I reminded her that, because of her excessive drinking, her children had come very close to being orphans. Maybe this miracle was a message to her to take stock of her lifestyle and reform her ways.

She listened thoughtfully, but her response was quite unexpected. "I guess it's a good thing I drink so much, eh!"

I was astounded. "How can you say that, Mary?" I asked. "Why is it a good thing you drink so much? Getting so drunk almost got you killed last night."

She was unperturbed by my disapproval and remained adamant. "Yes," she said. "It sure is a good thing I drink so much. If I hadn't been so drunk, I'd have sat up, and that bloody train would have taken my head right off."

Mary was not a flippant woman. This was said in the most sober tone of voice and serious mien, and without a hint of remorse. Her demeanour was grave, but her eyes were laughing. My lecture had not impressed her but neither had it offended her; it had amused her. Not only did she not believe me, but in her own unassertive way she was mocking me.

I missed the opportunity, if there ever had been an opportunity, to establish rapport and trust with Mary. Like every other white man she had known, I was condescending—I lectured her from the vantage point of superior morality and authority. She treated me like she treated all others who acted that way, with amused disdain. In her private opinion, I was just another reformer. She was right to doubt my story—she hadn't seen a train.

HE MISSED!

Saturday night in the city is the time for partying, for unwinding at the end of the week. Families and friends get together to socialize and quaff a few beers, recount the events of the week, and argue. The City Hospital was located in the core area of the city, and noted for its riotous Saturday nights. Weekend call was the proving ground for residents in the ER, surgery, anaesthesia, and ICU, where we learned our trade by full immersion. All too often, happy family parties turned into deadly brawls: mayhem and violence fuelled by a few too many beers. At times, our stalwart citizens resorted to lethal weapons, and the knifings, gunshot wounds, and beatings that resulted gave the on-call teams plenty of practice in the management of trauma and usually kept them busy well into Sunday.

Alex C. was a fairly typical example of Saturday-night celebrations gone awry. He was brought to the ER by ambulance, full lights and sirens, from a somewhat seedy area near the hospital. Initial assessment was started even as he was being wheeled into the trauma room. He was rapidly exsanguinating (losing blood) from what appeared to be a gunshot wound in the right side of his abdomen, just below the umbilicus. Although substantial external blood loss was obvious, we were sure there was much more inside his abdomen. He was on the verge of hemorrhagic shock: cold, clammy, vasoconstricted, with a thready pulse and undetectable blood pressure. No other signs of injury. At that moment a detailed history was unnecessary; the police would see to that. But, in any case, he was confused and incoherent, either from booze (the odour of which clung to him like dog hairs to a carpet) or shock. Our general assessment was brief. He appeared to be relatively young, about thirty, a little below average in size and fortunately in good physical condition. The sort of sport he had been indulging in was not well tolerated by the old and infirm.

Emergency treatment for this sort of trauma is pretty straightforward. First priority is to insert at least two or three of the largest intravenous cannulas possible, in whatever veins, peripheral or central, that can be located. The ER nurses and physicians are pretty good at this, and usually it's the nurse who gets the first line into the patient. From that point it's a struggle to transfuse enough saline, colloid, and emergency blood to keep ahead of the patient's ongoing internal blood loss until the operating room is ready. Surgical exploration is the definitive treatment.

The operating room (OR) was one floor above the ER. As we wheeled him out of the elevator, the OR nurses were counting the instruments, and the surgical residents were scrubbing. Careful induction of anaesthesia is critical in these cases; the wrong agent can kill the patient. That was the unfortunate experience when sodium pentothal was introduced to field anaesthesia at Pearl Harbor. It inhibits the reflex mechanisms that maintain circulation, and cardiac arrest quickly follows. Fortunately, ketamine had just been approved, and so ketamine, muscle relaxants, and an endotracheal tube had Alex ready for surgery in minutes.

A 12-gauge shotgun shell primed with #4 buckshot at close range can do a lot of damage. After the bleeding vessels had been located and ligated, there was a long night's work ahead to find the multiple holes in his bowel and repair or resect and re-examine. The surgical residents had plenty of practice in suturing bowel that night and well into Sunday.

I didn't get to see Alex again until Monday. Since I was the junior member of the team, it was left to me to complete the charting—that is, to record a proper history and physical examination. He was awake and conscious, though obviously painfully aware of an abdominal incision that extended from his xiphoid (the lower end of his sternum) to his pubis. (The surgical maxim is "big surgeon—big incision; small surgeon—small incision.") Although movement was particularly uncomfortable, he was in reasonably good humour and prepared to talk.

We got the usual pleasantries of introduction and past medical history over with fairly quickly. Then came the gist of the matter: How did he manage to get himself shot at close range by a 12-gauge shotgun? I didn't ask in those words, of course. I said something like, "Alex, do you remember being brought into the hospital?"

"No."

"Do you remember what you were doing Saturday night?"

This caused him to reflect a moment, but he nodded affirmatively.

"Do you remember getting shot?"

There was again a minute's hesitation. "Did I get shot?"

"Yes, Alex, you were shot in the belly. Tell me what you remember about Saturday night."

Alex thought for a minute, as if he were not accustomed to long speeches. "Well, my brother-in-law and me were having some beers, eh! We usually have a few beers and talk about hunting. I've known the bugger all my life, and we hunt together every fall." He stopped then as if that were the end of the story.

"Go on, Alex. What happened next?"

"Well, we got to arguing about who was the best shot, eh! I got to admit, I like my brother-in-law, but he can't shoot worth shit. I got all three bucks that we shot last year."

"Go on, Alex."

"Well, I told him that, and he got real mad. Said I was a lying little shit and he would kick my ass until it was up between my shoulder blades."

"Yes. Then what happened?"

"I didn't like that much, so I grabbed my hunting knife and told him, 'You try to kick my ass, you bugger, and I'll cut your balls off.'"

"Yes, and what did he do then?"

"Well, then he grabbed his shotgun and started waving it around and shouting at me, 'Don't you come any closer with that knife, you little shit. You take one more step and I'll blow your bloody head off.'"

"Yes, and then what happened?"

Then Alex did what I least expected at this point of his story. For a minute he looked puzzled, then, as his memory of the scene took shape, he started to grin, then to chortle, and then, desperately clutching a pillow to his belly, he laughed. It was not a polite laugh of appreciation, as if I'd said something funny; it was the explosive laugh of sudden comprehension—he just got the joke. When you laugh the first day after a major abdominal operation, it hurts. It doesn't just hurt; it is agonizingly painful. Your belly feels like it's coming open again. Alex hugged the pillow to his belly as tightly as he could and grimaced with pain, but it took some time before he regained control.

I was completely perplexed. "Alex, what's so funny? What the hell are you laughing about?"

He almost started to laugh again, but his belly was still on fire. Choking back his mirth, his reply clearly indicated that he was satisfied that he had won his point.

"The bugger was waving his shotgun around and shouting at me, 'You take one more step and I'll blow your bloody head off.' Well, I did, and he missed. I told you, he can't shoot worth shit."

THREE JEWISH DAUGHTERS

I begin this story with a tale of English daughters, not Jewish daughters. Shakespeare's King Lear had three daughters: Goneril, Regan, and Cordelia. The play begins with Lear's announcement that he intends to abdicate his throne and divide his kingdom among the three. But first they must declare their love for him. This was Lear's first tragic mistake, and it set the stage for a poisonous contest among his daughters for his love (and land). Lear's folly became the most famous of Shakespeare's tragedies; and his daughters' treachery led to the aged king's tragic humiliation, not the restful quiet for which he had wished. The motivations of all daughters in expressing their love for aging parents has ever since been suspect.

Lear's daughters were certainly not Jewish, but this play has a modern counterpart, intriguing though less tragic. Because my first impressions remain with me and are the most vivid, I have always considered the modern version a tale of three *Jewish* daughters. One example will suffice.

Mr. G. was an elderly gentleman in the advanced stages of metastatic cancer. He had been managing poorly at home, mainly because he was a widower with no immediate support, and he had developed several complications related to his disease and its treatment. The specific nature of these need not concern us. Finally, he was admitted to the chronic care unit (today it is more correctly called a *palliative care unit*) to stabilize his condition and adjust his medication. I was not his primary physician; in fact, I had just attached myself to the unit temporarily to learn something about palliative care. One thing I learned was that palliative care is as much about managing the family as it is about managing the patient.

Mr. G. owned a small retail business in an older part of the city. His business had a reputation for high quality and customer satisfaction. Although he was an active supporter of community charities and of his synagogue, he was not of that stratum of society whose names adorn the donor boards of hospitals and museums. I would describe him as one of the unpretentious, reliable, and generally unrewarded keepers of the community. He wasn't exactly King Lear, but he was a solid, respected citizen whose opinions were sought more often than they were offered. We would often spend extra time with him on rounds, because talking with him was a pleasant interlude from our more routine duties. It was thanks to this rather singular rapport that we obtained some insight into the disruptive behaviour of his daughters.

When he knew he had to go to the hospital, and without much prospect of leaving once he was there, he sent for his three daughters. On the second day after his admission, they all arrived. They had grown up in this city, and part of the reason for Mr. G.'s present modest circumstances was that he had sent them all to the best finishing schools. They had married well, their husbands were very successful litigation lawyers, and all now lived in the United States. Each of the daughters checked into a different hotel and each announced her arrival by phoning the head nurse on the ward. Each gave the nurse instructions to call immediately should there be any change in her father's condition and to have the attending physician phone her immediately with an update on her father's treatment.

We rarely saw these daughters. They came and went fleetingly and took pains to avoid each other. However, they more than compensated for their lack of physical presence by their domination of the telephone. The calls would begin about 10:00 a.m., when the first would call with a prepared list of questions; then the next would call with an almost identical list, and ditto for the third. The questions were almost never about Mr. G.'s general condition. They were about specific aspects of his treatment: what were his latest lab results; had his last laxative been effective; what time would the specialist see him today and could that specialist please phone her as soon as he finished? The same was repeated in the early afternoon, in the late afternoon, and in the evening. Each new bit of medical information was grist for a new round of questions and demands.

We all agree that patients' relatives should be kept informed, but this was going too far. The nursing staff and the house staff were going mad. They were on the telephone so much of the time that patient care, including that of Mr. G., was suffering. A polite suggestion that the daughters appoint one of their number as contact person had absolutely no effect on their behaviour.

We were desperate, and finally we turned to Mr. G. for help. Normally, we don't burden patients with this sort of problem, but we were at our wits' end and had exhausted the usual methods of persuasion. We began very delicately by noting that his daughters were unusually attentive and that they must have been very close to him since they spent so much time enquiring about his treatment. He just shook his head a little sadly and looked thoughtful for a few moments.

"The truth is," he said, "I haven't seen much of them in the past ten years, not since their mother's funeral. They're busy with their own lives, and they never did get on very well with each other. They were always trying to outdo each other, and each of them wants to be number one." He was describing typical sibling rivalry, of course. Like the daughters of Lear, these three were competing for their father's love, not for material but for emotional gain. Each carried a burden of guilt for her parental neglect; each was determined to prove that she was more loving than the others. The fact that they barely spoke to each other compounded the problem, but that was not unusual. Their fear of being left out of the picture gave us the key to their management.

Their father was a willing conspirator in the plan. All telephone enquiries were stopped and the daughters were offered exclusive access to the specialist on call but only as a group of three and only once a day. They accepted. The meetings usually took only an hour of the specialist's time, and the nurses were released to deal with the real issues of patient care. The daughters were still demanding, but now the situation was under better control.

I am intrigued by the origins of this behaviour. Is it the result of heredity or upbringing? Is it nature or nurture? My early encounters were with Jewish daughters, and I was convinced that this was a distinctive behaviour. This would fit well with a nurture theory, of the stereotypical Jewish-American princess who was nurtured by a typical guilt-inducing Jewish mother.[1] But in today's world, these stereotypes are harder to find and have less resonance. Other daughters, not always Jewish and not necessarily three, have acted in the same way.

Both stereotypes—the guilt-inducing Jewish mother and the spoiled Jewish-American princess daughter—are cultural myths, but they are firmly ingrained in American folklore and nurtured by a generation of Jewish comedians. Though amusing, they have limited value in explaining the behaviours of Mr. G.'s daughters.

If we discount the Jewish-American princess theory and accept that sibling rivalry between sisters exists in many cultures, we are left with the conclusion that its origins must be in nature, not nurture. It must be a hereditary trait common to all female *Homo sapiens*. In tribal societies, daughters, being less valued than sons, were forced to compete fiercely with each other for their parents' love and for the resources necessary for their survival. The most successful thrived, reproduced, and passed on the genes for this trait to their female offspring. This explanation firmly roots the behaviour in the realm of heredity —that is, nature rather than nurture.

Nowhere in his repertoire of plays does Shakespeare portray a Jewish-American princess. He offers no distracting, nurturing excuses for the selfishness of Goneril and Regan. It is assumed, without comment, that they were simply playing out the roles assigned to them by nature. Did a generation of American comedians disprove Shakespeare? I think not. Any father blessed with two or more daughters should go to the source and carefully read *King Lear*. Avoiding Lear's mistakes may be his only chance for happiness. The Jewish-American princess stereotype may be amusing to some people, but Lear's daughters are convincing.

At this point, a malicious reader may harbour the suspicion that I am a male chauvinist and anti-Semitic. Let me assure you that this would be a false assumption and that this story has a happy ending, an ending that casts doubt on both my theories. I spoke privately with only one of Mr. G.'s daughters, the youngest. Perhaps thinking that I had more influence than was actually the case, she took me into her confidence. "Is my father really dying?"

"Yes, though we can't say when," I replied quite truthfully, knowing that I was only confirming what she already knew.

"Could you let me know when it is close?" she said tearfully. "I would like to be with him. Please don't tell my sisters that I asked you, but you must arrange to have them called, too. If you don't, they will never forgive me."

I have witnessed much pathos in my career, and there was genuine pathos in her request. And, besides, even a hard-boiled doctor has difficulty refusing an elegant and distressed young woman who lays a trusting, finely manicured hand on his arm and asks a personal favour. Unwilling to admit my prior poor record in making these predictions and recognizing the real anguish in her voice, I agreed. But in the course of time, this scheme failed; Mr. G. survived beyond my short attachment to palliative care.

His last words to me were, "Doctor, do you think I spoiled them? Is this all my doing? They are all coming this afternoon, and I'm going to have a heart-to-heart talk with them." I have no account of their talk, but all three sisters were with him when he died. I doubt that Mr. G. had studied *King Lear*, but he recognized the causes of Lear's tragedy. Is this the modern version of the triumph of Cordelia over Goneril and Regan? In the end, do the bonds of parental love prevail over the satisfaction of outmanoeuvring your sisters? Was the reconciliation lasting? I cannot even speculate on these questions; I've never heard from them again.

JOE, WE NEED YOU!

W̶e milled about, laughing nervously, carefully selecting our seats, attempting to appear nonchalant. This was our first lecture in Theatre F of the old Basic Science Building, demolished in May 2017 in the larger scheme of the Rady Faculty of Health Sciences in Winnipeg. Even at that time, when we were students, it felt old, smelled old, and conjured up images of past grandeur. Later in life I visited the Ether Dome at the Massachusetts General Hospital, the site of the first successful demonstration of ether anaesthesia in 1846, and felt an eerie familiarity. But that demonstration in 1846, according to the single description that survives, was a raucous affair. We, the newly minted class of 1964, were subdued, and there was good reason for our anxiety: our lives were about to change in ways we could hardly imagine. Forty-five first-year medical students, forty-one men and four women, we were gathered for our first lecture in one of the fundamental medical sciences (along with anatomy and biochemistry) that made up the first-year curriculum. But we were not unprepared; we had been briefed by our older and more experienced comrades, those who had survived the first year. They assured us that physiology was the core of medicine, but they would rather face the Spanish Inquisition than repeat the course. We were to live, breathe, and dream physiology for the next year.

The initial impression of our professor was of a rather austere figure: tall, thin, and dressed in a plain black suit. This was belied by his laconic bearing. He sat on a bare wooden table, gazing up at his audience, idly smoking a cigarette. Perhaps *sat* is not quite the right description; he rested his right buttock on the table and his left foot on the floor, and he held his omnipresent cigarette in his left hand. During pauses, he flicked through the pages of a notebook with his right hand. Except for a piece of chalk, the notebook was his only prop. It was not his lecture notes; it contained the photos and names of the freshman class seated, oozing trepidation, on the rows of benches stretching above him. This was Physiology I, our introduction to medical science, and our lecturer was Professor Joe Doupe.[1] Though we interpreted his gaze as piercing and carefully searching for his targets, it may actually have reflected his difficulty in associating the faces above him with the photos in his book. Joe had severe diabetes, which he treated carelessly and which probably affected his vision. Perhaps that explained why he generally directed his questions to the front rows.

Joe Doupe was a teacher of the Socratic School. Now, Socrates is long dead and the Socratic method is known only from Plato's "Dialogues"; Socrates himself wrote nothing. In the "Dialogues" Plato describes Socrates's discussions with his friends in which he leads them, by systematic questioning, to new insights. The Socratic teacher does not lecture: he asks probing questions. The object is to guide the student towards a critical examination and thus a better understanding of his ideas. The Socratic method of enquiry does not presume that there is a final answer or an absolute truth; no statement is exempt from further questioning. And no topic is sacred, provided that the proposer is willing to expose his beliefs to critical scrutiny. It is the foundation of the scientific tradition, the basis for critical enquiry and the framework for the empiric system of reasoning.

Joe possessed a brilliant, insightful intellect, and his questions were penetrating. His lectures were brief and to the point. He used the blackboard only occasionally to highlight important points, but his critical questions were the catalyst for learning. Learning physiology with Joe was an exercise in self-discovery that strained our mental resources to their limits. His style became the intellectual foundation of the medical school, and he became a role model for hundreds of medical graduates. Even now, his shadow dominates the school, and, for us, it was a glimpse into the future.

When we graduated from Physiology I and finally from Medical School, we were convinced that we were the vanguard of a new intellectual revolution. We would complete the Age of Enlightenment begun by Francis Bacon and John Locke in the eighteenth century. Our world would be governed by reason and rationality. Science, based on critical enquiry, would show the way, and politics, religion, and economics would surely follow. The basic principles were simple: critical enquiry, intellectual honesty, and open and questioning minds. Science would lead us to a new Utopia. Such dreams! We were naïve, of course! Time, the great leveller, has tempered that idealism.

In a recent tribute to Joe, Dr. Arnold Naimark, former dean of Medicine and University of Manitoba president, said, "The independent mind is the guarantee of security from the tyranny of transient fashions." Joe exemplified the independent mind at work—his method was the foundation of our medical education. But perhaps he was the exception rather than the norm. Independent minds are usually at odds with the current trends. Is modern academia really based on respect for the independent mind, or is it based on the tyranny of transient fashion?

The evidence indicates that transient fashion, epitomized by the new social ideologies, has the upper hand. Marxist Leninism is still alive but is being challenged by gender diversity, social justice, feminism, and student rights. The ideologies vary from one university to another, depending upon which issues the faculty and student activists have found immediately compelling. But the reports are numerous enough to conclude that transient fashion is the new norm—often humorous but too often simply pathetic.

In a 2017 article published in the *Globe and Mail* entitled "Why Campuses Are Ditching Free Speech," author Margaret Wente reports that student activists at Wilfrid Laurier University, supported by faculty advisors, forced cancellation of a talk by a female lawyer who was prominently associated with the successful defence of a recent notorious sexual assault case.[2] The ironic reality is that she had not intended to talk about sexual assault but about the challenges facing women lawyers. Psychologists Greg Lukianoff and Jonathan Haidt have co-authored an illuminating review entitled "The Coddling of the American Mind," published in *The Atlantic*, and conclude: "In the name of emotional well-being, college students are increasingly demanding protection from words and ideas they don't like. Here's why that's disastrous for education—and mental health."[3]

Social media has made truth irrelevant, an insight beautifully summarized by Sarah Kedzior in another *Globe and Mail* editorial, entitled "At Long Last, a Forum Where Trump Cannot Escape the Truth": "It is not merely the message of the lie that matters, but its shameless delivery, as it implies that both public reaction and truth itself are irrelevant."[4]

Even those who want to defend the independent mind have bowed to public opinion. In yet another *Globe and Mail* opinion piece, entitled "Universities: Media Pool or Knowledge Centre," Eric Montpetit, professor of political science at the University of Montreal, writes: "In this post-truth period, in which falsities have become alternative facts in some circles, universities have a particular duty to protect their status as institutions that produce valid knowledge."[5] Unfortunately, the issue that Professor Montpetit has chosen to defend is another example of the university's choice of political correctness over freedom of discussion. The issue concerns an article written by Andrew Potter, entitled "How a Snowstorm Exposed Quebec's Real Problem: Social Malaise," for *Maclean's* magazine.[6] Admittedly, this article is socially controversial and treads on some very sensitive toes. It contravenes the self-image of many Quebecers that they are a socially distinct society, cohesive and self-sufficient. McGill University chose the politically easy path; it forced Potter to resign.

Our age of enlightenment is threatened now, just as it was in the Middle Ages, by a style of thinking that demands validation, not questioning, of current beliefs. Free speech, critical enquiry, and debate are being subjugated to political and social correctness.

"Not so," my ever-present djinn reminds me. "Are these not all good causes?" Who can dismiss social justice, gender diversity, the right of women to be respected and to receive equal pay? And, of course, my djinn is right. It is not the causes that are the problem, but it is the zeal of those who champion the causes. When a cause becomes sacrosanct, beyond questioning, beyond criticism, it becomes the transient fashion that Arnold Naimark has eloquently warned us against. When independent thinking and critical enquiry are most required, they are most resisted. Critics are suppressed, evidence is ignored, facts are irrelevant, and opponents are vilified. Freedom of enquiry is endangered today, just as it was in the pre-Enlightenment period.

This is a complex world we navigate. The choices described by Arnold Naimark still plague our universities and our society. Do we embrace the liberating power of the independent mind or the tyranny of transient fashion? Although a world in which everyone has an independent mind might be chaotic, everyone can have a critical mind. Our world needs more men and women who question, who never accept a statement without evidence, and who don't appease with easy solutions.

That was Joe's gift to his students and his university: an intellectual ideal, a system of critical thinking. But it is just one of many ideals that compete for the minds of students today—and it is not the most appealing. Critical thinking requires hard mental work and may be personally unpalatable. It requires reflection and questioning of one's own motives and beliefs, not just censure of the beliefs of others. An ideology that demands only conformity and allegiance to a cause and offers the security of group approval is much more attractive than an ideology that requires one to stand outside the group and question. World affairs and psychology have taught us the power of the mob and the appeal of transient fashion. History has shown that mob mentality and critical thinking are inimical.

Joe, your mission is not over; it has barely begun.

MORBID TALES
AND LESSONS FOR LIVING

THE LONGEST HALF-HOUR

During my penurious years of service as a junior medical officer in Her Majesty's Armed Forces, I moonlighted in the emergency room of a local community hospital. It was a small hospital, and the ER doctor on the night shift also covered the ICU. Since the worst disasters went directly to the General Hospital, which was larger and better staffed, most of our ER work was routine. Occasionally, however, a serious emergency would arrive that we had to admit. When that happened on my shift, I would have to cope with both the ER and ICU until morning. That was the case the night Mr. A. arrived.

Mr. A. was rushed to the ER, crumpled in the back seat of the family sedan, after collapsing at home. His was a classic history. A robust working man of about fifty years, in good health except for hypertension, he suddenly cried out that his head was splitting and fell to the floor. Although he had been mumbling incoherently when they carried him to the car, he was comatose on arrival at the hospital. This was long before CT (computed tomography) and MRI (magnetic resonance imaging) scans were available. Probably it was completely unnecessary, but I did a quick lumbar puncture to confirm that there was fresh blood in his cerebrospinal fluid. I'm not sure now whether it was done to allay my anxiety or strengthen my case when talking with his family. In either case I wanted to be certain of my diagnosis that he had had a massive intracranial hemorrhage and the prognosis was hopeless.

He was quickly shifted to the ICU for observation. Meanwhile, the number of anxious relatives now overflowing our tiny waiting room was swelling. As delicately as was possible, I prepared them for the worst, his teenage daughter acting as my interpreter. There was little hope to offer them. It was my considered opinion that he would not live through the night. The message may have come through more bluntly in the interpretation than was intended, and it triggered a chorus of wails and tears that continued unabated. As the number in attendance increased, so did the volume. The relatives must have derived some comfort from each other's company, because they left Mr. A. entirely to the care of the ICU nurses. Perhaps they realized that the sheer weight and volume of their support were the best they could do.

There was little more I could do, so I returned to the ER, where there was now a substantial backlog. Even there we could still hear the weeping of the grieving family.

The ICU nurses knew their jobs well and kept me posted with updates on Mr. A.'s condition. When he became totally unresponsive to painful stimulation, I was sure the end must be near. By now the disruptions of his noisy and restless retinue were beginning to grate on our nerves. When he developed Cheyne-Stokes breathing (irregular breathing), I briefly considered the life-support options we could provide but immediately dismissed the notion. There was no need to write Do Not Resuscitate or Comfort Measures Only orders. The nurses knew what to do and were not about to initiate futile attempts at CPR. That was just as well, because the ER had become even busier and I had little time to devote to a hopeless case. Their family priest had arrived, and he was quietly advised to administer the last rites. When the nurses finally called to inform me that Mr. A. had stopped breathing, I was relieved, hoping that this would bring the denouement to the tragic drama that was disrupting the routine of our small hospital.

My quick examination indicated absence of both respiration and radial pulse. I wanted to get the most unpleasant duty over first—that is, to inform the family of his demise. Locating the immediate family members was easier than extracting them from their clinging support group, but eventually a nurse and I got them into a small private room where we could be heard. As expected, they were devastated, and their crescendo of grief was enough to transmit the message to the others. For several minutes anguish prevailed. Now they wanted to see him. Perhaps it was a premonition that held me back, the hot breath of my omnipresent genie on the back of my neck. I hesitated and said, "Just give the nurses a few minutes to make him look better."

While I was sitting at the nursing station, completing his death certificate, my genie struck. The practical nurse who was tidying the body for family viewing darted out of the room with a look and manner that I had come to recognize presaged trouble. "You'd better come back quickly," she said, "he's still breathing." When my re-examination confirmed her report, the full impact of my situation hit me. The nurse was mostly right; he wasn't exactly breathing, but he was gasping at a rate of three to four breaths per minute: agonal breathing. And they weren't gasps that could be ignored: they reverberated in that small room, accompanied by a heaving chest and flaring nostrils. Moreover, he had a clearly palpable femoral pulse, something I had not checked before. It should have been obvious to any fool that he was not dead; no lay person stepping into that room would have had a moment's doubt. Within moments his grieving family would expose me as just that fool.

I have since seen many patients dying from neurological causes and have come to understand that the exact timing is uncertain and the physical signs deceptive. The clusters of neurons in the medullary part of the brain that control breathing and heartbeat do not shut off like an electrical switch; they wind down like a potter's wheel. Agonal gasping can continue for minutes, sometimes hours. If the heart is basically healthy, it requires only a little oxygen in order to keep beating, and I have seen strong hearts continue to contract for thirty minutes after breathing has ceased entirely. Blood pressure, pulse rate, and force of cardiac contraction vary unpredictably. Electrical activity of the heart, the ECG, may continue long after pulse and heart sounds have ceased.

The reasons for my misjudgment were not my immediate concern; I feared that I was on the verge of more than just embarrassment. The noisy throng milling in the corridor were a sturdy lot of bricklayers and plasterers. They were of an ethnic origin noted for volatility and mistrust of official institutions. When they discovered that their dear brother, whom I had just declared dead, was perceptibly alive, I wanted to be far away. It would be uncomfortable enough to be identified as the perpetrator of a morbid hoax, but, more seriously, they might conclude that his treatment had been careless.

I needed time, and the first necessity was to divert the approaching wife and children. Nurses were dispatched to delay them by any means, using any excuses necessary. With the door firmly closed and locked, I had time to consider my plight. What were my options? One: I could slip out the back door and leave town. Two: I could admit my error and face the consequences, but I knew that he would die soon and my humiliation might be averted. Three: I could hold a pillow over his face until he stopped breathing, but my good intentions might be misinterpreted. Four: I could sweat it out.

The next thirty minutes were among the longest of my life. I counted each gasp, I waited, and I pondered. The garbled voices on the other side of the door also subsided, as if they, too, were waiting. In expectation? For what? For a miracle? There were patients who needed me in the ER, but they could also wait. It was a time for reflection: How did I get into this awful mess?

There were three presences in the room. There was poor Mr. A., brain dead, gasping his last few breaths. He could not be blamed; after all, his was the greater loss. There was me, a victim of circumstance. And there was my ever-present djinn. He chuckled; he was the only winner—he had tripped me up again.

"How did you get me this time?"

"It was easy, young Dr. Tweed. You committed the cardinal sins of medicine."

"But I did all the right things at the right time. This man's fate was sealed before I touched him."

"Ah, yes, but you tripped yourself. You forgot that lack of skill or knowledge is seldom the cause of a doctor's errors. You were distracted, thinking about the patients waiting to be seen rather than the one in front of you. And you were presumptuous; you presumed he was lifeless and that's what you saw. You were hasty, in a hurry to get back to those you could treat, and rushed your examination of the one you could not. And your greatest sin was hubris: overconfidence, not questioning your own judgment, relying on your first impressions."

He was right. I had set the trap; he had merely sprung it. My penance was to wait it out.

When there had been no gasps and no pulse for a full fifteen minutes, I came out. His family was restive and didn't understand my strange ritual. I was thankful that they were respectful enough not to enquire. It was the nursing staff who saved my reputation. I never learned what they told the wife and children that kept them pacified for half an hour, or how they explained my need to be alone with the patient for so long. But they made it appear as if it were part of the routine, and hospital routine is inviolate.

Now, when I am called to pronounce a patient dead, I get very busy. For at least half an hour, I am engrossed in another task, cannot be located, or become urgently engaged. After all, on a scale that stretches to eternity, it makes little difference if the patient's official departure time is delayed for half an hour. I have never forgotten that a half-hour can seem like an eternity.

THE ABSURDITY OF LIFE

This is a story about suicide, about a specific suicide. It shocked everyone in the hospital, even the battle-hardened ER nurses. Suicide both repels us and intrigues us—it is horrifying and repugnant, but it is also dramatic and fascinating. We have all seen the riveting images of someone jumping off a bridge or poised on a window ledge twenty storeys above the street. That is the public-news bite, but the pathos is seldom visible.

On reflection, we find it difficult to imagine a life totally devoid of joy and hope, a life so meaningless, futile, and unbearable that suicide is a logical choice. Very few of us have been there, but many of us have encountered suffering souls who have faced that dilemma. What forces them to decide that suicide is the only solution?

One hot afternoon late in the summer of 1965, I was the junior intern in the ER of the City Hospital. I was not only the junior intern but also the only, and therefore the senior, physician in the ER that afternoon. The ER was our proving ground, the front line for all the mayhem, violence, tragedy, and despair of the city. Fortunately, few cases were as tragic and pathetic as the one I describe here.

The oppressive heat of the afternoon had just abated when the paramedic team called to warn us that they were bringing in a patient who had been brutally mutilated. There were few details. Apparently, she had been attacked in her small apartment, where she also carried on business as a seamstress. A late-afternoon customer had found her and called the police. The only evidence that might identify her assailant was a pair of bloodstained tailor's shears, found on the floor beside her. The police hoped there would be fingerprints on the shears. She had said nothing to them except to request that someone call the Humane Society to collect her cat.

At first glance there was nothing particularly remarkable about the patient: she was conscious but withdrawn, perhaps in her mid-thirties, had plain but regular features, was overweight, and was not in any obvious distress. In fact, considering the report we had received, her affect was remarkably flat and unperturbed.

Only when we removed the sheet covering her torso did we realize the severity of her injuries. Her abdomen had been viciously slashed, and much of her bowel was extruded. The bowel that was visible had also been cut across in several places. It is not easy to open a person's abdomen; ask any surgeon. Even with a sharp scalpel, a surgeon has to incise several layers, and it takes determination, dexterity, and time. This was obviously the work of a determined assailant.

When we had completely removed the sheet, more was revealed. She had an indwelling urinary catheter, and both her legs were withered. She was paraplegic, had been for some time, and lived and worked from a wheelchair. All this had already been noted by the paramedics and police. It was the identity and motive of her attacker that had them puzzled. Apparently, she lived alone and had no obvious enemies and no immediate family or friends, and there were no signs of a struggle.

There was, in reality, little that we could do for her in the ER. We started an intravenous drip to replenish her lost blood and fluids, called the surgical service, and arranged for her admission to the ward. It was not until I was well into the mundane details of admission that I recognized the obvious. She had neither complained of pain nor asked for pain medication. She was not only paraplegic but was totally anaesthetic (without sensation) from the rib cage down.

It was now clear to us that this injury was not a vicious assault; it was self-inflicted. But the methodical care with which she attacked her abdomen had confused us. She had apparently disembowelled herself with a pair of sharp tailor's shears just as if she were cutting a piece of wool serge for an overcoat. The method she had chosen was without doubt brutally effective;

since neither the abdominal wall nor the bowel had sensation, she was able to do it carefully and deliberately.

The surgical team took several hours to identify and repair all the tears in her bowel and to close her abdomen, but it was all in vain. She got her wish and died of septic shock from peritonitis three days later in the ICU. No visitors came to comfort her.

This happened over fifty years ago, and her face still haunts me. Is suicide in such a brutal yet systematic way impulsive or carefully planned? Was she depressed, or was this a rational decision? Was it a last, desperate attempt for autonomy in a life in which she had lost control, or was it a desperate plea for attention?

I am of that genre of doctors educated in a very traditional system. We have sworn the Hippocratic Oath and earned our public trust as defenders of life. The very core of our professional values is the assumption that every human life has worth. To deliberately discard life in this manner contradicts all our beliefs, and we have difficulty comprehending what sort of life is so devoid of meaning as to justify this treatment.

I have struggled with these contradictions for most of my career, and I still do not have a satisfactory answer. Recently, the essays of Albert Camus have helped me to view suicide and assisted suicide more sympathetically, though I recognize that I cannot share the victim's emotions and despair.

Albert Camus (1913–1960) experienced first-hand the senseless brutality of both the Algerian struggles for independence and the Nazi occupation of France during World War II. During the war he was an active supporter of the French Resistance as an underground journalist, and at various periods he was also an anarchist, communist, and social activist. His writings distilled the public mood of the period. In 1957 he was awarded the Nobel Prize for Literature "for his important literary production, which with clear-sighted earnestness illuminates the problems of the human conscience in our times."[1]

One of Camus's essays, *The Myth of Sisyphus,* is devoted to a philosophical discussion of suicide and begins with the statement "There is but one truly serious philosophical problem, and that is suicide. Judging whether life is or is not worth living amounts to answering the fundamental question of philosophy."[2]

Sisyphus was a mythical Greek king who annoyed the gods with his pranks, most egregiously by preying on his guests. This sin particularly angered Zeus, the god of hospitality. The punishment of Sisyphus was, for all eternity, to roll a boulder up a mountain only to have it roll back down again each time. His punishment encapsulates the idea of eternal futility, and Camus calls him "the absurd hero."

Camus expanded on this classical theme in his idea of the *absurd*, which probably reflected the chaos of the world in which he lived. *Absurd* is a good word to describe the longing for meaning and clarity in a world that seems to offer neither. In Camus's philosophy, life *per se* has no intrinsic or sacred value; it is the experiences of living that give it meaning. He framed the philosophical idea of the *paradox of the absurd* as a contrast between our expectation that life should have meaning and significance and the harsh reality that despair and mortality are our only sure reward. This leads to a philosophical question: If life has no meaning and no value, is suicide logically justifiable? In such a world is it a rational decision to choose death over hope?

Camus did not discuss the special case of the terminally ill, but, on philosophical grounds, he rejected suicide as a general solution to the absurdity of life, not because he valued life but because he opposed nihilism. Death does not confer meaning to life. Suicide is the ultimate negation, the decisive act of nihilism that extinguishes both life and hope.

Let us now fast forward to 2018, when physician-assisted suicide is our liberator—and the issue is not the ethics of suicide but the guidelines by which patients are to be screened for euthanasia. The preferred term now is *medical assistance in dying* (MAiD), perhaps a less threatening term than *euthanasia* but with the same intent. MAiD has forced us to rethink old concepts about the value of life; a more personal view of suicide is emerging, one that portrays it as a gentle and welcome release. This is an issue that may transform our culture. We are discarding reverence for the intrinsic value of life, but are we satisfied with the hedonistic alternative? Is the value of living to be measured only by the pleasure it permits?

Now we can rephrase the question posed earlier: Are there circumstances in which suicide is a rational solution to the absurdity of life? We have already discarded the ethics of the past, which were based on a theological construct that has no traction in today's society. Having accepted that life has no *a priori* intrinsic or sacred value, we return to Camus. Life is significant only for the experiences it offers. The variety and satisfaction of those experiences define the *value of life*, and the absurdity is the paradox of expectations versus reality.

By redefining life in social rather than theological terms, we make suicide acceptable and permit an ethical role for physicians. We must remember, though, that absurdity does not demand death. Sisyphus did not consider suicide, and Camus objected to suicide as a nihilistic solution that extinguishes both life and hope. There are no examples of nihilism in medicine other than suicide, and, philosophically, nihilism and medicine are not good companions.

The decision for MAiD, or to request MAiD, is not just a response to the absurdity of living. It may also be an attempt to assert autonomy in the final closing of the curtain, to avoid the uncertainties about end-of-life care. Perhaps some who are terminally ill might prefer the certainty of a gentle, welcome death over the uncertainty of the alternatives. If this were true, palliative-care proponents (and that includes me) face a challenge in public relations. The slogan "dying with dignity" has been linked so often with assisted suicide that they are considered inseparable. Patients who choose palliative care must be reassured that natural death in an atmosphere of comfort, love, acceptance, peace, and even gratitude is also dignified.

Euthanasia and palliative care are at the opposite poles of a spectrum of treatment, with many nuances in between. The role of opioid narcotics, such as morphine, in palliative care illustrates one of those nuances. Morphine is, without question, the most useful end-of-life medication we possess. It not only relieves pain but also induces a mild euphoria that relieves the anxiety of dying. However, morphine also has its side effects; the dose needed to relieve pain may depress breathing and circulation. And this is the dilemma: achieving the primary intent, which is to relieve suffering, may also shorten life. But this is not medical assistance in dying; ending life is not the primary intent.

I doubt that our patient had read Camus, but she lived the absurdity that he described. Her violent self-mutilation may have been her last attempt to draw attention to her misery. If she had had the option, would she have preferred a more gentle and peaceful death? We can't know. We know only that she had lost control over many aspects of her life, and she ended it in the most brutal way imaginable. This story is her legacy and our lesson in humanity.

Both ethics and our humanity demand that we not judge the motives or actions of someone like the seamstress. Our ethical aims as physicians are the same today as when I graduated. We are bound to relieve pain and suffering and observe the utmost respect for human life. Respect for life does not require that we persist in futile efforts to prolong life, and neither does it demand that we deny compassionate treatment that may shorten life. But does it condone giving drugs with the primary intent of ending life? That is the ethical dilemma that MAiD has unleashed, and it will plague physicians for many years.

On that score I side with Camus, and the seamstress has certainly helped shape my attitudes. Suicide is an act of nihilism, extinguishing both life and hope. I cannot imagine a life so absurd that hope is completely lost, but I recognize that my view is conditioned by my experiences. Others will have had different experiences and different attitudes, and as I age and develop the infirmities of age, my attitudes will change. Perhaps I will come to value life, and the small pleasures it offers, even more. Perhaps living will become absurd, or perhaps I will be too senile to know the difference. Each of us must find our own path.

A TIME TO DIE

The wisdom literature of our cultural roots often provides remarkable insight into current issues. We are now in the midst of a national discussion, particularly challenging to the medical profession, about choosing our time to die. This is a very old question, addressed in the twenty-first book of the Old Testament (Ecclesiastes 3:1–8) in a passage often quoted at funerals: "To everything there is a season, and a time to every purpose . . . a time to be born and a time to die. . . ." In Ecclesiastes, our role and tasks are defined by divine order, and the time to die is part of God's plan. The right time is when our appointed tasks are finished, when we have fulfilled our role in creation. But this is not much different from the evolutionary world view where our place in the natural order and time of dying are also determined for us, not by a divine plan but by random selection. Both theology and evolutionary science describe a natural order, a cycle of life, and a time when that cycle is complete. This acceptance of life and death as part of the natural order was brought home to me by one of my most memorable patients, Mrs. Lena B.

I was a junior resident on the medical service of the City Hospital in the autumn of 1970. We admitted an elderly woman from the ER to a medical bed, mainly because no other place would take her. Hospital admission was not her choice; it was our only option. Scant information came with her. She had lived alone in a small apartment and had managed, in a way, until then. A neighbour who looked in on her had called an ambulance because Mrs. Lena B. could not, or would not, get out of bed. We had no other medical history and, even with an interpreter, were unable to elicit anything of significance. However, bit by bit, we were able to piece together a social history.

Lena B. was a survivor; she had survived both poverty and persecution. During the Stalin era, she had escaped from the 1932–33 famine in Ukraine, walked for days carrying her two children, and eventually got to Sweden. Her husband had been "drafted" into a work camp, and she didn't see him again for almost ten years. Eventually, she made her way to Canada and eked out a living working in a factory. It was enough of a living to educate her children, keep her husband supplied with cigarettes and a little whiskey, and just barely sustain herself. Now, her husband long dead, her children widely dispersed, she lived like many other elderly widows, her church and a few old acquaintances her only interests.

Lena did not actively resist our efforts to get her out of her bed, but she simply would not cooperate. She did not converse, eat, or drink. She was passive and seemingly unaware of our attempts to stimulate her. Since she had no identifiable medical condition other than advanced age, there was nothing to treat. Tube feeding and intravenous fluids were considered, but we didn't have a diagnosis that justified forced feeding. We had no permission to intervene, and we were uncertain about what to do. A diagnosis of depression was also considered, but there had been no signs of that prior to her current admission.

Lena died quietly on about the eighth day after admission, having had no medical diagnosis or active treatment. The cause of death was recorded as heart failure due to advanced age.

In the years since, I have often questioned our decision not to intervene more aggressively in Lena's care. However, at the time, her disinterest in living seemed clear, and aggressive intervention looked to us more like assault than treatment. In retrospect, I believe that her life and death were the embodiment of Ecclesiastes: her tasks had been accomplished; the cycle had been completed. She knew it was her time and accepted her fate with resignation and dignity. She didn't actively seek death; she simply stopped living. We respected her wishes as we saw, or thought we saw, them.

Lena was a unique patient, but her actions posed a larger question: How, in a civilized society, if old age and redundancy make life intolerable, can one end it gracefully without incurring the stigma of suicide?

Though medical attitudes toward death and dying have undergone dramatic changes since 1970, the answer to this question still eludes us. Medical assistance in dying (MAiD) is now legally available for the terminally ill, for conditions that are "grievous and irredeemable." This describes old age, but *old age* does not qualify. The disease must be deemed "an advanced stage of irreversible decline." This, too, describes old age, but *old age* does not qualify. We must also consider whether natural death is "reasonably foreseeable." That again describes old age, but *old age* does not qualify. "Enduring suffering that is intolerable to the individual" is a necessary criterion, but the level of suffering that is intolerable is a personal decision. Most restrictive, however, is the requirement that the applicant be mentally competent and give voluntary consent. The senescence of old age therefore disqualifies many of our elderly from consenting, even if they otherwise qualify.

Lena would have quickly been excluded from consideration; she did not meet any of these criteria except, perhaps, that of *intolerable suffering*. But it was a very private suffering, not the sort that was evident to her attending physicians.

Another option available today is the *advance directive*, which states our wishes and preferences when we become terminally ill and/or mentally incapacitated. Currently, an advance directive can specify only what is *not* to be done (e.g., no CPR, no intubation, no intensive care). When a patient is not mentally competent to give consent, most medical institutions will respect their advance directive, either written or orally expressed. However, there is no provision in advanced directives to request MAiD on a contingency basis or any other treatment that contravenes established medical practice. If Lena had written an advance directive, it would probably have been honoured. Lacking that and any other instructions, we assumed, based on her disinterest in living, that those were her wishes.

Can we guess the future? I believe there will be more emphasis on advance directives—essentially end-of-life instructions—that reflect one's personal autonomy and the right to decide one's own fate. In my imagination I see myself writing these instructions: "When I have reached an age when I do not appreciate the company of family and friends, when I have lost interest in living, too mentally incapacitated to consent, I instruct you to euthanize me." But the question is: Who is the *you*? Who will make the decision that it is time for me to go? Certainly, in order to protect the vulnerable person (me, in this case), it should not be someone who would gain from my death. This would exclude my doctor (because my doctor would get a fee and be rid of a nuisance), and my family and my beneficiaries. In fact, it would exclude almost everyone I know. The only arrangement that I can imagine that would protect my vulnerability would be to pay a disinterested third party a fee every three months to examine me and pronounce me *ready* or *not ready*. But, in order to continue collecting fees, it would be in the best interests of that person to pronounce me *not ready* and thereby collect the next quarterly fee. His or her interests would therefore counterbalance the interests of those who might benefit from my departure.

Since Ecclesiastes was written, we have come a long way in our thinking about the time to die. There are many who are kept alive beyond their "appointed" time, and there are others who will be assisted to die in advance of their "appointed" time. Lena B. was an exception, not the rule, but her choice gave us a glimpse of the present and the future. The time to die can now be framed as a personal decision. We can indicate our preferences by writing advance directives, though we cannot yet be certain that they will be honoured. My fantasy directive would be ridiculed if presented now. But who knows what the future holds? I'll tuck it away with my other papers.

TO LIVE LONG
OR TO LIVE WELL?

In the early years of intensive care, *failure to wean* was a nightmare for ICU physicians. I don't mean *weaning* in the usual sense: that is, weaning from attachment to the mother's breast. Rather, *weaning* in the medical sense is weaning from dependency on what was intended to be a temporary treatment. Opioid analgesics are currently the popular example. When I was an ICU physician, *dependency* usually meant dependency on an artificial ventilator, and *failure to wean* meant that the patient could not breathe without the ventilator.

In some circumstances dependency is to be expected and accepted; for example, poliomyelitis or high spinal-cord injury with respiratory-muscle paralysis might cause respiratory failure that leaves a patient ventilator-dependent, perhaps for life. But, at the time I worked in the ICU, the more common and troublesome failures to wean were self-induced, mainly from chronic bronchitis and emphysema caused by cigarette smoking. There were other causes, of course: pneumoconiosis from working in the coal or asbestos mines, and cystic fibrosis, for example. But the cigarette was our main culprit.

Chronic lung disease due to cigarette smoking comes in two guises: "pink puffers" and "blue bloaters." Pink puffers (emphysematous) are usually thin, cachectic, barrel-chested individuals who feel short of breath (dyspneic) and compensate by puffing (hyperventilating). As a result, they usually maintain adequate blood oxygen levels and consequently look pink. Blue bloaters (those with chronic bronchitis) have right-heart failure and bloating (edematous swelling) and look blue (cyanotic) because they have more red cells but carry less oxygen in their blood than the pink puffers do. Pink puffers are generally more dyspneic but better compensated.

Mrs. N. was a pink puffer. She had earned it by fifty pack-years of cigarette smoking (a pack a day for fifty years, or two packs for twenty-five years) and was in an advanced stage of emphysema. She could no longer consistently maintain adequate blood oxygen levels by puffing, and her blood carbon-dioxide levels would also rise. When this happened she became severely dyspneic and would be brought to the ER, intubated, and placed on artificial ventilation for two to three days. In her previous admissions she had improved each time, had been successfully weaned, and had gone home. But her home leaves were becoming shorter, and, with each admission, weaning became more difficult.

On a sunny Monday morning in the spring of 1978, I arrived on H7, the intensive care ward of the City Hospital, to find Mrs. N. occupying her usual cubicle, sedated and on full ventilator support. I expected a visit from her sons that afternoon. Dealing with her sons was part of the challenge of caring for Mrs. N. She was a widow, and her two sons were both prominent young specialists in our hospital, one of them three to four years my senior. Both were extremely careful not to interfere in their mother's care, but they were very attentive and were always kept very well informed about her treatment. They were a close-knit family, and we strove to accommodate their wishes.

Her ventilator care proceeded as usual, but after about a week there was no improvement. Several attempts to wean her from the ventilator had failed; she had become too distressed to continue breathing. It was beginning to look like the dreaded failure-to-wean scenario. We concluded that her disease had progressed too far and that she simply didn't have enough functioning lung left to breathe.

Her sons sensed our unease and became even more attentive. They, too, could see that she had made no progress in the previous week. Though too polite to insist, they clearly expected an explanation. It was time for a serious talk.

Failure to wean is a disaster in many ways. It is demoralizing for the ICU staff but even more so for the family and the patient.

In our previous experience, patients with end-stage respiratory disease who could not be weaned, like Mrs. N., never left the ICU. They died in one or two or three weeks from pneumonia, sepsis, or organ failure. It was an unpleasant, exasperating, and emotionally draining experience for all concerned.

I met with Bill and Dave, and we started with some small talk—doctor talk (a variation on jock talk). Then I outlined their mother's prognosis as I saw it. It was my opinion, expressed perhaps with a little more certainty than my experience warranted, that she would not wean this time and would not leave the ICU alive.

Bill and Dave understood; they had been warned of this eventuality. They didn't want their mother to suffer unnecessarily, but there was no other treatment for her condition. I stressed our shared feeling of helplessness when all that is left to do is to relieve suffering. We had much in common; as neurologists, they were often faced with a similar predicament, one in which they could diagnose a neurological disease but had no treatment to offer.

I suggested that they have a meeting with their mother. Without seeming to be too grim, I could see only one course for her. Yes, the ventilator was keeping her alive, but as the days went on, her life and theirs would get increasingly intolerable. The treatment we could offer, although the best available at the time, would not reverse her disease. She could, if that were her wish, ask that the endotracheal tube and ventilator be removed. I did not insist that they tell her she would probably die soon after, though I was sure she understood. We all agreed it had to be her decision, and I was careful not to interfere in their discussion. It was not a long discussion; she had already made her choice.

I also promised Bill and Dave that a dash of morphine (one to two milligrams intravenously at regular intervals) would relieve her sensation of dyspnea and make her last hours as comfortable as possible. Morphine, though a respiratory depressant and normally never given to patients in respiratory failure, is a mainstay of symptom relief in terminal care. We all, staff and family, understood that comfort measures would be maintained—nursing care, supplemental oxygen, and intravenous fluids—but we would not reintubate her or do CPR. It was not necessary to write this as DNR orders; they were understood implicitly.

We were pleased with our preparations to make her comfortable. Mrs. N. was given a private room down a hallway, where her family could have unlimited access. She asked for her own pyjamas and housecoat and discarded the hospital garb. Her sons brought flowers and pictures to brighten up her room and make it look like home. When all were gathered, I removed the ventilator, and when she started to breathe again, I removed the endotracheal tube. Though her breathing was laboured, for the first time in several days she could talk, one or two words at a time. My last act was to inject some morphine intravenously, and when she was comfortable I left, not to spare myself but because my part was finished.

The next morning, I arrived fully expecting to find her bed empty and all traces of her gone. To my surprise (and admittedly some chagrin), she was still there, semi-conscious and puffing at a rate of ten to twelve breaths per minute. Her family had spent most of the night with her and had noted her slight improvement. They were discreet as always; no one questioned my earlier caution that she would not live until morning.

The next day she was more awake and puffing at her usual rate. She looked no better and no worse than when she had been admitted. Since her family had been spending their days and nights in the hospital and we were not treating her actively, I suggested that they take her home.

That was the last I saw of Mrs. N. To my great surprise, she lived at home for about another six months. I learned that she had died quietly in her bed. I met Bill and Dave occasionally in the hospital corridors. They were always polite and genial, but they never discussed their mother. I am still baffled. Was this my most miserable failure or a medical success?

It is the duty, the obligation, of a physician to inform patients and family about the possible outcomes of treatment. But what if one is wrong? Was I conveying certainty when no such certainty was warranted? Were my expectations influenced by her smoking habit and my general pessimism about smoking and lung disease?

I was certainly humbled, and my enthusiasm for predicting outcomes—especially life-and-death outcomes—was decidedly dampened. But had it been the right course after all? Would she have died in the ICU as I predicted and our decision to back off prolonged her life? Could I justifiably claim that my treatment was correct, though the outcome was not what I had expected? My malign and ever-vigilant genie just chuckled; he had won again.

But self-justification is not my reason for telling this story. We are all fallible, and judgment is seldom perfect. This story is not about me, but, rather, it is about a woman who taught me two important medical lessons. One is that the likelihood that a medical prognosis will be wrong varies directly with the confidence with which it has been pronounced. A life-or-death prognosis pronounced with grave confidence to many listeners (especially relatives) will certainly be proven wrong.

The other, more important, lesson was about quality of life. She, and her sons, understood the alternatives and the consequences of each choice; she was asked to choose between a few hours of independence and relative comfort or several weeks of futile dependency and distress. This was not a theoretical option; it was her commitment to what she considered most important. She had no hesitation; she chose to live well rather than live longer, to salvage a few hours of quality time. She was rewarded with more, but that was not anticipated.

This is a decision with which we might all eventually struggle. I hope we can do it with her courage and equanimity.

A BEATING HEART
IN A WARM CORPSE

Donald George Junor was taken to an operating room of the City Hospital on July 26, 1975, to remove his kidneys for transplantation into another patient. My description of him as "a beating heart in a warm corpse" was not, of course, his medical diagnosis but was part of my evidence given several months later at the trial of Louis George Adams and Clifford James Kitching, the two men accused of killing him. The medical diagnosis was "traumatic brain injury with irreversible coma." *Irreversible coma* was a new concept developed specifically to identify suitable organ donors. We shall see that this was a concept that challenged the conventional wisdom of the time.[1]

The case created a local sensation, and the trial was widely reported. Both accused were represented by very able lawyers, Robert Tapper and Greg Brodsky, who contended that it had been the doctors, not their clients, who had killed Donald Junor, and the motive was to harvest his kidneys. I was the chief medical witness and was tasked with defending our actions in terms understandable to the court and to the public. Mr. Brodsky had asked me a simple but basic question: "Was Corporal Junor alive or dead when you removed his kidneys?" The correct answer, which would have confused everyone, would have been that he was neither completely alive nor completely dead. I did not want to tread there.

My goal was to persuade a skeptical jury that Cpl. Junor was killed by the actions of the two bouncers who had dragged him from the bar that night. And the members of the jury had good reason to be skeptical. The common understanding at that time was that a beating heart was the cardinal sign of life and life ceased when the heart ceased to beat. I had to convince the jurors that the life and identity of Cpl. Junor resided in his brain and ceased when his brain permanently ceased to function, though his heart continued to beat until after his kidneys were removed. More generally, I was arguing that the *vital principle* of life resides in the brain, not the heart.

An article written by Anne Marie Travers and published in the *Winnipeg Tribune* tells the story as seen by the press and public. The article captures the drama but Cpl. Junor, the person, is forgotten. This is not how he should be remembered. Now, forty years later, I would like to tell his story from my point of view.

Donald Junor was a twenty-six-year-old soldier, home on leave in the midsummer of 1975. On the night of July 24, he was drinking alone in a bar in the old garment district of Winnipeg. Not only was he drinking alone but he drank to the point of unconsciousness. We know little about his personal life, or why it ended in those sordid circumstances. He was not a derelict; he was a serving soldier, a corporal in the Princess Patricia's Canadian Light Infantry regiment then stationed in Esquimalt, British Columbia.[2]

Cpl. Junor passed out about midnight in the Vibrations Discotheque of the St. Charles Hotel, which, in its Edwardian grandeur, still stands proudly at the corner of Notre Dame Avenue and Albert Street. The two bouncers on trial, in an astounding act of callous indifference, lifted him by the armpits, dragged him up the stairs, and dropped him face down on the sidewalk of Albert Street. A taxi driver parked at the curb testified that it sounded like an egg hitting the concrete. Of course, a conscious person would have reflexively lifted his head and taken the impact with his chest and arms. Cpl. Junor had no protective reflexes; his head hit the concrete like a melon dropped from a truck.

When he arrived at the hospital, two things were quickly established: first, he was drunk, with a blood alcohol level three times what was then considered too drunk to drive; second, he had a massive traumatic brain injury with rapidly progressive

Heart kept going 'in warm corpse'

By Anne Marie Travers
Tribune Staff Writer

After Donald George Junor's condition was declared "irreversible," doctors kept his heart beating — not with the hope of saving his life, but to preserve the health of his kidneys for transplant, testimony at a manslaughter trial revealed Thursday.

Dr. Arnold Tweed, who officially pronounced Mr. Junor dead July 25, testified, the victim was in an "irreversible coma" when his heart beat was temporarily restored for the sole purpose of keeping his kidney alive.

An anaesthetist at the Health Sciences Centre, Dr. Tweed told an assize court jury, "when Mr. Junor was taken to the operating room for removal of his kidney it was my opinion he was dead . . . that we were simply maintaining a heart beat in a warm corpse."

His testimony was made on the fourth day of the trial of Louis George Adams and Clifford James Kitching, two young Winnipeg men who pleaded not guilty to manslaughter in the death of Mr. Junor.

The two men admitted to police they dragged Mr. Junor out of the Vibrations Discotheque, 22 Albert St. on July 24 and dropped him face down on the sidewalk, court was told earlier this week.

Mr. Junor, a 27-year-old serviceman was taken to hospital where he died the next day.

Dr. Tweed told the court that on his first examination of Mr. Junor he determined "he was suffering a brain injury as a result of a blow to his head."

He said blood samples revealed "Mr. Junor was severely intoxicated (at time of death) perhaps to the point of being unconscious as a result of alcohol."

On his third examination he found "Mr. Junor had a complete absence of function at any level of his brain from the highest to the lowest levels," the court was told.

Mr. Junor suffered a cardiac arrest July 25, which "in ordinary circumstances I would have considered the end point," said Dr. Tweed.

"We were satisifed his outlook for recovery was absolutely hopeless."

However, court was told, a relative had granted permission for the donation of Mr. Junor's kidneys, so he was put on a respirator, operated on and then disconnected from the artificial breathing machine.

Under cross-examination by defence lawyer Greg Brodsky, Dr. Tweed said he filled out the formal death certificate in the case, and added it is hospital policy to do this after — not before — a transport.

Mr. Brodsky suggested to the witness that a formal declaration of death should be made before a transplant to avoid the risk of being accused of removing an organ from a person who is not yet dead.

Dr. Tweed said this procedure was strictly a matter of policy decided by individual hospital boards and was immaterial.

"Mr. Junor was already dead when his kidney's were removed. " He said Mr. Junor's condition that of an "irreversible coma" — was recorded on hospital charts and that "the whole question is one of semantics."

In a lengthy elaboration to the court he said, "dying is a process, not an event." "A doctor has to decide at what point of time the dying process is irreversible."

He said if he had his choice he'd wait until the point of decomposition to declare death — "it would be the most safe" — "but society doesn't permit that."

In Mr. Junor's case, Dr. Tweed said "I determined his dying process had become irreversible." "We could have kept his heart beating artificially but we couldn't reverse the process."

Mr. Brodsky asked if Mr. Junor's heart could have been kept beating after his kidney was removed if the respirator had not been unplugged.

Dr. Tweed said "possibly, for a very short period of time."

The court was told Dr. Tweed is a specialist in anaesthesia; is on the staff of the intensive care unit at the Health Sciences Centre and has done extensive research on brain injury.

Dr. Neil Donan also appeared as medical witness for the Crown Thursday. Also on staff in the intensive care unit, Dr. Donan told the court his job is to resuscitate patients brought into the emergency department.

He testified that when Mr. Junor was brought in July 24 he noted no respiration, no pulse, and no heart activity. He administered external cardiac massage and certain drug doses, and after hooked Mr. Junor up to a respirator, or breathing bag. Seven minutes after this treatment, spontaneous respiration was restored, said Dr. Donan.

Asked under cross-examination if in his opinion Mr. Junor was dead on arrival at the hospital, Dr. Donan said "there was no pulse and no respiration — it depends on what is defined as death." "You should speak to someone more qualified than me to define death."

He testified marks he noted on Mr. Junor's neck "looked like stretch marks," and added they were "quite superfical." He also called skin abrasions he noted on Mr. Junor's face, "superficial", and said "I have no idea how much force was required to cause them."

The trial was to continue today in the Court of Queen's Bench.

Winnipeg Tribune, March 26, 1976

brain swelling and hemorrhage. Within hours it was apparent that his brain damage was lethal.

When we took Cpl. Junor to the operating room two days later to harvest his kidneys, he was not officially dead. According to the criteria and terminology used then, known as the *Harvard Criteria*, he was in a state of "irreversible coma." The time of clinical death, when I signed his death certificate, was after his kidneys had been removed, after we had stopped the ventilator that breathed for him, and after his heart had stopped beating.

It was the ambiguity between irreversible coma and death that caused me much discomfort at the trial of his assailants. In justifying our actions it was necessary for me to make two arguments that would be understood by the jurors: first, that dying was a process, not an event; and second, that irreversible coma marked a stage in the process when there was no possibility of recovery. The defence used the same clinical facts to argue that Cpl. Junor was alive when his kidneys were removed and that stopping the ventilator was the immediate cause of death. They argued that the doctors, not their clients, were the immediate agents of his demise.

Life and death are the Siamese twins of our existence, inseparable from the moment of conception. After several millennia of careful observation, we should have no difficulty in distinguishing one from the other. But, as with Siamese twins, they may have certain resemblances and occasionally one may mimic the other. For example, deep hypothermia can make the living appear dead and modern intensive care can make the dead appear to be alive.

This uncertainty about the boundaries between life and death is founded in philosophical and theological constructs— belief in a *vital principle* of life, or *life force* that is distinct from the physical soma of the individual. The belief in separation of soul and body was virtually universal in earlier times and is still prevalent. Western society generally followed the Catholic doctrine that the vital principle (or soul) entered the body at conception and left at death. However, there was no clear agreement about where it resided in the body and at what point in the dying process it left. Probably the most common belief was that it resided in the heart and left when the heart ceased to beat.[3]

This conclusion was supported by the medical observation of the time that, after decapitation or hanging, the heart continued to beat for several minutes after all other vital functions had ceased. The beating heart as both the symbol and embodiment of life is thus firmly engrained in Western culture.

If we believe that the vital principle of life resides in a beating heart, certification of death must wait until all vital signs are extinguished: breathing, reflexes, and heartbeat. Since all physicians are aware that heartbeat may persist for some time after other vital functions have ceased, prudence urges one to be slow and methodical. Haste may punish the unwary.

Two advances in medical science—life-support intensive care and organ transplantation—forced the profession to re-examine the traditional approach. The historical criteria—that is, complete absence of any signs of life—became an obstacle to medical progress in these fields.

Life-support intensive care, which owes its origins to poliomyelitis and the iron lung, changed our understanding of the dying process. Poliomyelitis was aptly called *infantile paralysis* because the worst cases have ascending muscle paralysis, which may include the respiratory muscles. Before there were intensive care units, those with respiratory paralysis usually died. The Drinker negative-pressure respirator, better known as the *iron lung*, was first used at the Boston Children's Hospital in 1928 and the Hospital for Sick Children in Toronto in 1937. It rescued many who would otherwise have died. In Manitoba these machines were introduced in the municipal hospitals during the polio epidemic of 1953, the worst of several dreaded epidemics before polio vaccine became available.

The iron lung, though a brutally cumbersome machine, inaugurated a new era in medical care and a eureka moment in conceptual thinking about life and death. One of our vital functions—breathing—could be replaced by a machine. This has now been extended to both circulation (heart–lung bypass) and kidney function (dialysis). Hearts that have arrested can be restarted, and patients with lethal head injuries and strokes can be kept "alive" in classical terms for days or even weeks. But as yet we have no substitute for the functions of the human brain.

The first successful kidney transplant—successful in terms of long-term survival—was performed at the Brigham Hospital in Boston in 1954 by Dr. Joseph Murray (1919–2012). He received the Nobel Prize for Medicine in 1990 for his contributions to organ transplantation. The transplant was successful mainly because the donor was a living identical twin and the donor kidney was immediately transplanted into his brother. This circumvented the two major complications that cause a transplanted kidney to fail: immune rejection and ischemic injury prior to harvesting. Within a very few years, rejection yielded to tissue typing and immune-suppressant drugs, and the supply of viable donor kidneys became the limiting factor.

The largest pool for healthy transplantable organs is beating-heart donors. This pool is mainly populated by young people who have had lethal head injuries; we credit the motorcycle as our most consistent supplier. But, although the beating heart is necessary to keep the kidney healthy until it is harvested, it is also the major obstacle to public acceptance. A beating heart is a sign of life. A new concept of death and dying was needed.

The first breakthrough came from the Harvard Medical School, the cradle of transplant surgery. In 1968 the Harvard Ad Hoc Committee on Brain Death published their diagnostic criteria for the total and irreversible arrest of all brain functions, a strict set of neurological tests to establish that a patient was a potential organ donor.[4] However, although their mandate was to study brain death, they chose to call this state *irreversible coma,* implying that the state of functional impairment was both total and irreversible. It was their criteria that we were using in July 1975.

At that time, *irreversible coma* was a new concept for doctors, lawyers, and certainly the public. We recognized clinical death (permanent cessation of all vital functions) and biologic death (decomposition), but this was a new idea and not easy to understand. Coma was something like deep sleep, but how could we be certain that it was irreversible?

The description of Cpl. Junor as a "beating heart in a warm corpse" was my attempt at a graphical image that would convince the jury that dying is a process and not an event. Irreversible coma is a step in that process, and without life support, all other vital functions will quickly fail. Even with life support there is only a short window of opportunity when vital organs are still healthy and can be harvested for transplantation.

This was an important conceptual shift, but it still left a lingering uncertainty. The argument about irreversible coma as a step in a process was too complicated, too obtuse. A more satisfactory solution came by a simple analogy with traditional thinking. If permanent cessation of heartbeat was accepted as cardiac death, then permanent cessation of brain function must be brain death, and both are precursors to biological death of all other tissues and organs. In both cases, the vital principle has abandoned the body. Both allow a window of opportunity, longer with brain death, when healthy organs can be harvested.

The Manitoba legislature, in its Vital Statistics Act of 1975, provided the first statutory definition of death in Canada: "The death of a person takes place at the time at which irreversible cessation of all that person's brain function occurs." In 1981 the Law Reform Commission of Canada recommended that Parliament enact this provision in the Interpretation Act.

You might say that this is just semantics, that we are describing the same condition but with different words. That is true, but this change has produced a clarity that has permitted transplant programs to flourish. Many people have had their lives restored by kidneys, hearts, livers, and lungs from unfortunate donors who were "brain dead" and had no more use for the organs.

Modern medical science has resolved the age-old debate. We have established that the centre of identity, of conscious awareness, of everything that makes us individual, lies in the brain, not in the heart. In spiritual terms one might say that we have located the vital principle of life in the brain. All other organs of the body are ancillary and replaceable.

When I discovered the newspaper clipping in my files and began to think about this story, I searched for a closure that would adequately express our debt to Cpl. Junor. By coincidence, he and I had played our parts in a significant period of medical history, though his was the tragic role. Medical and social change go together and always follow a similar pattern. Technical expertise is always achieved first; professional and public acceptance follow at a much slower pace. Acceptance of transformative medical interventions often requires revision of established social attitudes and values.

This was the case for both intensive care and organ transplantation. Neither could achieve their full potential until social attitudes toward living and dying had changed. The same could be said for therapeutic abortion and now for medical assistance in dying. Beliefs about the sanctity of life continue to change.

Before I could submit his story to public scrutiny, I needed to reconnect with Cpl. Junor. I needed to recapture some of the ambience associated with these events and to test the authenticity of my memories. I also wanted to see what visible legacy history had assigned him. His burial site was easy to find on an Internet registry. Glenyce and I visited his grave on a warm August afternoon in 2016, a little more than forty-one years after the events I have described.

The municipal cemetery in Estevan, Saskatchewan, is located on a gently sloping hillside at the north edge of the city. Cpl. Junor is buried in the military section, near the top of the slope. This location is prime cemetery real estate with good *feng shui:* a pleasant view, soothing breezes, and gentle drainage. The gravestone is inscribed in simple military format: regimental number, rank, name, and dates. It will remain long after the other details of this episode have faded from memory.

Grave of Cpl. Donald George Junor, age 26, City of Estevan cemetery, Estevan, Saskatchewan

No soldier chooses to die in the service of his country, but many do. No soldier can choose the time, place, and circumstances of his dying. These are not considered relevant when we honour a dead soldier; we believe that all who die in the service of their country deserve equal respect. Donald Junor did not choose to be killed in a sordid midnight tragedy outside a sleazy nightclub, but in his dying he served his countrymen in a manner he could never have anticipated. His legacy, for those who care to inquire, is inscribed on his gravestone. Cpl. Donald George Junor was a soldier; he is buried in a soldier's grave, and this story is a tribute to his sacrifice.

MEDICAL MYSTERIES, PRAYER, AND PROVIDENCE

SUSPENDED ANIMATION

A tough school for tough kids! That was how you would have described St. John's Cathedral Boys' School in the 1970s. It was a denominational school located on the banks of the Red River about eight kilometres north of Selkirk, Manitoba. Many of its students were boys whose misdirected energy had led them adrift in the public-school system. School programs at St. John's were based on the principle of "muscular Christianity," in which the boys' self-esteem was rebuilt by pushing them to their physical limits of endurance. They were tested with gruelling outdoor events: punishing 800-kilometre canoe trips in the summer, fifty-kilometre snowshoe races and dogsled runs in mid-winter. It was a school that prided itself on building "character," and its successes were notable, as were its failures. The need to achieve was so compelling that even those whose physical abilities were not equal to these extreme challenges would continue until they collapsed.[1]

On January 31, 1976, sixteen-year-old Edward Milligan was not able to complete his forty-kilometre snowshoe race. He collapsed in the snow about two kilometres from the finish line, wet with sweat, exhausted and hypothermic. When he was delivered to the emergency room of the Selkirk General Hospital about ninety minutes later, he was clinically dead. The doctor on duty, Dr. Robert Smith, could detect no signs of life; there were no responses, no breathing, no heartbeat, and the body was cold, below twenty-five degrees Centigrade. The ambulance attendants had made roughly the same observations and had performed CPR *en route*. With this information any sensible doctor would have turned his efforts to consoling the parents. But it was Edward's good fortune that Dr. Smith and Dr. Gerry Bristow, who had arrived about the same time, were not sensible doctors. Something about this boy, possibly the cold,

Edward Milligan, early February 1976

puzzled and disturbed them. They continued CPR and began to warm Ed's body. Within about an hour they were rewarded; his heart began to quiver, and with further CPR and defibrillation it started to beat. He had been in documented cardiac arrest for eighty-five minutes, and restoration of heartbeat carried no certainty that his brain had survived. They worried that they had resuscitated a heart but not a person.

I saw him early next morning, after his transfer to the ICU at the City Hospital. Within a few hours he started to breathe spontaneously, and by afternoon he was conscious. From that point on, his recovery was marred only by some minor frostbite. When interviewed several weeks later, he was mentally normal and happy to forget his ordeal.[2]

Later we learned that it was the longest recorded episode of cardiac arrest with complete recovery. This case attracted much attention and some imitators. Winnipeg soon became known as a world centre for treatment of hypothermic cardiac arrest. The usual victims had gotten drunk, started walking home, and had fallen asleep in a snowdrift. One young woman whom we came to know well, Sally B., was resuscitated three times in two years after falling drunk into the snow. Over the course of time, she lost bits and pieces to frostbite—some fingers, toes, and the tips of her nose and ears—but not her good-natured optimism. Each time she recovered she was bright and cheerful and promised faithfully never to drink again. Then she stopped coming to us, and I must assume she kept her promise.

Bodies not alive but not quite dead, suspended between life and death (a state known now as *suspended animation*)—this is the stuff of mythology and science fiction. It is undoubtedly the most puzzling and fascinating of the medical mysteries and has stirred the imaginations of futurists, scientists, and generations of cryo-preservation wishful thinkers. Time has not diminished its mystique, and it is currently being seriously studied by NASA and by respected universities.

The earliest written description of suspended animation may be the myth of the handsome shepherd boy Endymion and the moon goddess Diana. Jupiter recognized Diana's infatuation for the comely shepherd boy and bestowed on him perpetual youth and perpetual sleep so that Diana, being immortal, of course, could lie with him forever.

Shakespeare used suspended animation as a dramatic effect in several plays. The best known is *Romeo and Juliet,* in which Juliet takes a potion to induce a stupor resembling death, so realistic a simulation that Romeo takes her for dead and commits suicide. In *The Winter's Tale,* Hermione, wife of Leontes, is suspended for sixteen years as an unfinished statue. In fairy tales the theme of suspended animation is found in the stories of *Sleeping Beauty* and *Rip van Winkle.* In Hollywood it has featured in several sci-fi epics, including *2001, A Space Odyssey* and, in 2016, *Passengers.*

Suspended animation fascinates both spiritualists and scientists. What transpires in the mind during this period of suspended life? If the individual has a soul, is it in the body, leaving the body, or is it outside the body? Are there medical applications? What is the potential for space travel and time travel?

Musings about the restless soul, as in near-death and out-of-body experiences, are entertaining but not of much scientific value. Stories like that of Ed Milligan are of more interest to the medical community and suggest the practical applications.

Deep hypothermia has been used to facilitate both open-heart surgery and complex neurosurgery. Dr. Wilfred G. Bigelow, who was born and raised in Brandon, Manitoba, and graduated in medicine from the University of Toronto, was one of the pioneers of open-heart cardiac surgery. He understood that cardiac surgeons could effectively repair intracardiac defects only if they could see what they were doing, and for that they had to have a bloodless operating field and a still heart in which to work. It was daring, but it worked. Deep hypothermia permitted a period of cardiac arrest long enough to do a complex surgical repair with the confidence that the patient would survive with mental functions intact. Bigelow pioneered the experimental work, and his technique, which permitted operating "in the heart" to repair damaged valves and congenital defects, was the key, for which he was awarded the Order of Canada. The citation describes him as "an internationally acclaimed pioneer of hypothermia in heart surgery."

In Winnipeg Dr. Dwight Parkinson pioneered a technique to repair arterio-venous malformations deep in the brain (carotid-cavernous sinus fistulae) under deep hypothermia. Patients' core temperatures were reduced to about eighteen degrees Centigrade, the heart was stopped, and Dr. Parkinson had a perfectly bloodless brain to work with for about forty-five minutes.

However, medical science moves quickly, and these early applications are now of only historical interest. Cardiopulmonary bypass and interventional radiology (stenting, coiling, and embolization techniques) have made it unnecessary to stop circulation, and now the only application of hypothermia in cardiac surgery is local cooling of the heart during cardiopulmonary bypass.

Why hypothermia? It is not the only way to protect the brain, but it is the most effective. How does it work? The chemical explanation is known as the *Arrhenius equation*, proposed by Svante Arrhenius in 1889. Simply stated, chemical reaction rates are temperature-dependent. The metabolism of the brain follows the same rule. A decrease in body temperature of ten degrees Centigrade roughly halves metabolic processes in the body and perhaps a bit more in the brain. This is enough to increase the time the brain will tolerate complete ischemia from five minutes to about forty minutes. The chemistry is wonderfully consistent over a wide range of temperature, and it is tempting to speculate: For how long could we extend this state by decreasing temperature to, say, zero degrees, or even -273 degrees, Centigrade?

Unfortunately, the answer to date is—we can't. Temperatures as low as about twelve degrees with survival have been recorded, but not lower. Humans are not natural hibernators, and human tissue does not survive freezing. But human embryos have been preserved for years, and viable DNA has been recovered from the mastodons. Perhaps this is our clue, and perhaps we should look to our DNA for the secrets of immortality. In 1996 a Finn–Dorset sheep named Dolly was the first animal successfully cloned from the DNA of another animal of the same species. Although my body will decay, my DNA could be preserved for long after I am dead. But, of course, my clone wouldn't be me; he would be my much younger, identical, twin. Like any identical twin he would be his own person. On second thought, I will spare him that burden; better to start life with a new body rather than with my handicaps.

But as quickly as one use fades, others appear: space travel, cryopreservation, transplant medicine, and more. Science does not advance on hesitation. Successful innovation in science is the exploration of fantasy, and this is illustrated by NASA's plans to invest research money and talent in a project they call "Torpor Inducing Transfer Habitat for Human Stasis to Mars." The logistics of space travel would be greatly simplified by putting most of the crew in hypothermic-induced suspended animation for the journey. This is preliminary research for the Mars mission, about a nine-month return journey. How close are we to seeing this? The Mars mission is targeted for the 2030s, and the limiting factor is clearly human endurance, not space technology.

On the medical front the Safar Center for Resuscitation Research at the University of Pittsburgh (named after resuscitation pioneer Peter Safar) continues with groundbreaking research. Their projects include hypothermia-induced suspended animation for victims of lethal trauma as well as for neonatal asphyxia and cardiac arrest. The object is to buy time and prevent further injury until definitive treatment can be reached. Clinical trials have been encouraging, but medicine is, like the stock market, difficult to predict.

Does suspended animation provide the key to medical and cosmic breakthroughs? Our limitations lie not in our imaginations but in our physiology. Human dreams may extend beyond the heavens and the grave, but evolution has given us a body that is bound to the earth. Our biologic equipment is good for about a century, our brain requires a constant supply of oxygen, and we don't keep well when deprived of our earthly comforts. Random selection has made us both superior and vulnerable. Perhaps Ed Milligan's recovery tested the limits of human resilience.

But science is optimistic, and we refuse to admit limits. Our future on earth may look grim, but we clutch at hope; we can dream that suspended animation might enable us to avoid our evolutionary destiny of extinction and death. It might permit us to escape from this earth to another universe when we have made Earth uninhabitable. Or it could be a way for those left behind to survive the next Ice Age. On the other hand, these ideas could be just pipe dreams. The science of suspended animation may have reached a "glass wall." We can see the tantalizing shadows beyond the wall, but we are unable to penetrate it. Just as well! If these fantasies were to succeed, the survivors would awaken in strange, unfamiliar, and probably hostile worlds.

Despite my appreciation for science fiction, I prefer to stay firmly planted on Earth and enjoy my suspended animation in small doses and familiar surroundings: a glass of single-malt scotch, a wood fire, some Beethoven, and my life's companion beside me. The evolutionary triumph of the human brain, what makes us truly distinct, is that our cosmos can be entirely internal. We don't have to physically touch the stars in order to know them.

NEAR-DEATH EXPERIENCES

To look death in the eye and at the last moment to be pulled back is an immensely moving experience. It is no surprise that many who have been that close to dying have fantastic stories to tell. Each story is unique, but there is a commonality among them, now widely known as the *near-death experience* (NDE). Medical scientists—psychiatrists, psychologists, and neuroscientists—have struggled to find explanations for the NDE that fit a medical model. Spiritualists insist that the NDE is the wandering of a conscious soul that is leaving the dying body to seek another world but is called back. To date, neither side has proved its case or disproved the other.

Today's hi-tech medical interventions have made the NDE more common, and vivid reports engage a growing audience: literally a cult following that has thousands of cases recorded on one Website alone (NDERF.org). Books and articles on this topic, often based on personal experiences, overflow bookshelves. One can participate in national conferences and attend a week-long course to simulate the NDE.

Brian's Story

With so much hype, you would suspect that these reports are pure hoax. But you get a different impression when you talk with someone who has been there. Brian Moore is one of them. He is an intelligent and practical man, a successful businessman and municipal politician. Now seventy-four years of age, he has been a member of the Anglican Church all his life and a regular churchgoer. But when asked about his beliefs, he admits he had been skeptical about heaven, hell, and an afterlife. That is, until September 26, 2015. This is his story of that day as told to me about two years later.

We talked in his office in the building-supply centre that he owns. Brian looked up from his laptop when I entered, leaned over his desk, and stuck out his hand as if I were the most welcome visitor he'd had all day. He was a bit hazy on the medical details, as expected, but the rest of his story needed no prompting. He struggled at times to find words to describe the extraordinary images and feelings that he'd experienced, but the clarity had not faded. This is a common difficulty, and some call these experiences *ineffable*—that is, literally beyond our powers of description. Here's how Brian describes the events:

> The day started much like any other working day. I was helping a customer load cinder blocks onto his truck, perhaps a bit too strenuous a job for a man of my age. Not that I had any health concerns; I still did a full day's work. However, when I got back to my desk, sitting in my chair, catching my breath, I was seized with the worst pain I have ever felt—a crushing chest pain that left me cold and sweating. I called out to my secretary, and after one look at me, she called the ambulance.
>
> Fortunately, we live in a small town—Killarney, Manitoba—and within about fifteen minutes I was in the hospital's emergency room. The doctor on call checked my pulse and blood pressure, then immediately put in a call to the senior hospital doctor, Dr. Anton Pio. I remember both her urgency and the voice of Dr. Pio as he answered his phone. My next conscious memory was waking up in St. Boniface Hospital in Winnipeg, several hours later.

A lot happened during those hours, events that changed Brian's life. This is what he has pieced together from the reports of his doctors and nurses:

> I'd had a cardiac arrest; my heart had stopped for ten minutes. They did CPR—chest compressions—and other measures to restart my heart, including eight electric shocks [defibrillations]. And they called the air ambulance to medevac me to the cardiac unit at St. Boniface Hospital in Winnipeg. Later I was told they didn't expect I would make it alive; I was unconscious the whole way. In the hospital, I guess, I went

directly to the cardiac room, where they found a complete occlusion of the main artery supplying the left side of my heart. Fortunately, they were able to stent it successfully. I don't remember any of this. My first conscious recollection is waking up in my hospital bed, but I do have vivid recollections of visions (I don't know what else to call them) in which I was outside my body at least part of this time.

Brian describes his NDE this way:

At some point between hearing Dr. Pio's voice in Killarney and awakening in St. Boniface Hospital, I sensed I was in a tunnel. It felt like I was at one end of a tunnel and floating up. The tunnel was dark, but the walls were brilliant, a kaleidoscope of colour. At the top was a dazzling white light, and as I approached it, the light got brighter. I didn't believe a light could be so bright. Not only did it get brighter but it also began to radiate warmth and love. I felt loved; I didn't want to go back.

But I guess I did come back; I recall looking down at myself. I could see the outline of my body; I'm sure it was my body even though I couldn't make out the face. I was black or in shadow, lying on my back with arms outstretched above the head.

To me the visions were real, very real, not just dreams. I knew that the body was mine, though I couldn't see the face. The light, I am sure, was God, and the closer I got, the more I could feel His presence.

On his third day in hospital Brian had another vision:

It was evening. I was lying awake when suddenly the end wall of my room became bright-blue sky. A golden ball went across that sky, trailing a golden streak. Again, this was lucid and vivid, and I believe it was God's reminder to me that I had been saved for a purpose.

This was definitely a life-changing experience. When I was young I was terrified of death, not just of my own death but also of the death of my parents. When I was five or six years old, I would wake up crying. My mother would comfort me and ask what was wrong, but I never told her that I was dreaming of dying. Now, after having this near-death experience, I have totally lost my fear of death. I'm not in a hurry to go, but I have no dread of the prospect. I am thankful for the life I have been given and am sure that there is a god and an afterlife. What form they take, I do not know, but I have experienced the welcome that they offer.

The experience has changed my understanding of my purpose on earth and my goals during my remaining years. I am more thankful for the blessings of life, and I believe I am more understanding and tolerant. At first I was reluctant to talk about my NDE—I didn't even know the term then—but my church and other neighbouring churches, as well as community groups, have asked me to share my experience with them. A few weeks ago I was invited to talk to the congregation of a small Mennonite church in a nearby town, Mather, Manitoba. After the service, an old Mennonite gentleman, not somebody I knew, sought me out. He shook my hand, thanked me, and said that my talk had given him great comfort. Three weeks later I was surprised to hear that he had died; he hadn't told me he had terminal cancer.

I have thought about this man and his gratitude and have begun to wonder: If my message was a comfort to him, could it not also be a comfort to others who are near dying? Should I be less reticent about sharing my experience? Was giving comfort and hope the mission for which I was spared?

Although each NDE story has its individual peculiarities, they share remarkable similarities. Brian's account is typical. Most describe the experience as remarkably vivid and realistic—not like a dream—and very much a positive, life-changing event.

Neurosurgeon Eben Alexander's very popular bestseller, *Proof of Heaven*,[1] is currently the most colourful and detailed personal story of an NDE. Alexander was stricken with bacterial meningitis in 2008. A confirmatory statement from his physician establishes the medical facts: Eben was in a coma for six days, and his recovery was remarkable, if not miraculous.

He describes two sets of visions. The first is a set of out-of-body experiences, which he describes, with absolute conviction, as journeys to heaven and back. He passed through three realms: a murky transitional zone (a state of limbo), a gateway (brilliantly lit, with celestial music and lush landscape), and heaven itself, dominated by a core of intelligent light (revealing God or OM). He was able to communicate non-verbally with God through his young female companion, who, in this realm, took the form of an orb. Alexander claims these visions occurred during the depth of his coma but has no confirmatory evidence, other than his convictions. The other set of visions was clearly part of awaking—visions of a worldly nature associated with past experiences in his life. These he dismisses as fantasy.

Alexander's claim for the veracity of his experience is that he has moved the plane of perception from "real" to "ultra-real." His visions are proof of an afterlife, absolute and uncontestable, too real to be questioned. They also make for entertaining reading.

About 10 to 20 per cent of people resuscitated from cardiac arrest report a near-death vision, and about 80 per cent of those describe the event in positive terms associated with feelings of detachment, levitation, serenity, security, warmth, light, and love. Recognition of ancestors or spiritual figures and reluctance to return to the body are common. Those who have had positive experiences believe they have been changed for the better and report enhanced love of life, serenity, tolerance, and a more charitable outlook. We would like to understand these transformative experiences better, but where do we begin?

One approach to understanding the unfamiliar is to make a comparison with the familiar. We all carry a set of vivid memories, memories of the surprising, dramatic, and dangerous events of our lives. These are usually emotionally charged events that have deep personal significance—a parent's death, a car accident, or a near miss—and they often pop up in our minds unbidden. Psychologists have named this type of memory *flashbulb memory*.[2] Recall of a flashbulb memory usually recaptures both the details and the emotional aura of the original incident. Almost everyone in my generation can remember the day John F. Kennedy was assassinated—where we were, what we were doing, and the feelings of shock and disbelief we had. The same holds true for the 9/11 attacks; just say "9/11" and everyone can recall the appalling pictures of passenger jets crashing into the World Trade Center.

Are NDEs just another type of flashbulb memory? If so, they are much more complex. Flashbulb memories are anchored in space and time. They can be spatially fixed by reference to concrete objects in the surroundings, by time, and by independent observers. An NDE has none of those. The visual images of an NDE are otherworldly; the sense of time is distorted and independent corroboration is impossible. Although those who have had an NDE report it as real, they are describing a reality that cannot be confirmed by veridical evidence.

Most investigators who have studied these phenomena are not primarily concerned with the accuracy of recall; their interests lie in the mysteries of their origin and meaning. The psychological explanation is that these are dissociative mental states or states of consciousness that fall under the general categories of dreams, delirium, or hallucination. In the psychological model they unquestionably arise from the brain and can be imitated by certain drugs: for example, the anaesthetic drug ketamine.

The spiritual explanation is that they are transcendent experiences, psychic or paranormal evidence of duality of soul and body. Those people with strong spiritual beliefs see them as proof of the existence of a soul, of an afterlife, and of God and heaven. This is not a scientific proof, of course; it is an intuitive proof. Intuitive proofs are ideas felt so strongly, so clearly and with such surety that they cannot be denied. Intuitive certainties need not conform to logic, and therefore scientific attempts to confirm or reject them are irrelevant.

Skeptics scoff at the spiritual explanation. To claim these visions as proof of anything offends the non-believer's intuitive certainty that science will eventually explain everything that needs to be known about life and death.

But both skeptics and believers, busily defending their own intuitive certainties, have missed the key point: these are transformative personal experiences. Their value is not that they support one world view or another, but it is in the personal benefits—the change in values and outlook—that accrue to the one who has had the experience.

In determining the worth of an NDE, we all work from the same page: the personal account. Those of us who have not had such an experience must listen to those who have; there is no other way to study NDEs. They are never described as *abstract notions* but are highly significant individual experiences that have profound personal meaning and consequences.

Many who have experienced an NDE report changes in their intuitive understanding of life and death. One remarkable consequence reported by almost all, including Brian, is complete loss of the fear of dying. Those who have had an NDE do not invite death, but they no longer dread it. They interpret their NDE as assurance of a continued existence, though the form of that existence remains a mystery. Brian, like many others, is pragmatic and accepts some degree of uncertainty in all these matters, but he is grateful for the extension of his mortal existence and not afraid of the next.

Is there any benefit for the rest of us poor souls who have not been privileged with the experience? I am quite prepared to share these marvellous insights with them, vicariously, of course. Attempting to provoke a real NDE is too dangerous a game for me.

Some Research

Several authors have catalogued experiences such as Brian's and identified the features that set them apart. Raymond A. Moody, an American philosopher, medical doctor, and psychiatrist, gets the credit for coining the term *near-death experience* and, through his writing and lectures, for popularizing the phenomenon. His unusual combination of academic credentials gave the topic scientific credibility. He published his first findings in 1975, and his most recent book, entitled *Life after Life* (2015), describes a large collection of NDE reports and a catalogue of common features. He recognizes that personal significance is the real value: "More than academic and professional issues are involved. [A near-death experience] involves deeply personal issues, for what we learn about death may make an important difference in the way we live our lives."[3]

William James, one of the most influential American scholars of the late nineteenth century, said much the same. In *The Varieties of Religious Experience*,[4] written in 1902, he stated that a revelation or transformational experience could be judged objectively only by its effects. He also insisted that we judge the contribution of the experience by human standards of value, by its contribution to human welfare. If the effect had been beneficial—that is, if the recipient became a better and happier person, or if there had been a benefit to society—it was a valuable experience.

In 1998 Jeffrey Long founded the Near-Death Experience Research Foundation. Since then he has collected thousands of reports on its website (NDERF.org) and has described them in his recent book, *Evidence of the Afterlife*.[5] He has identified twelve basic elements of an NDE, though very few of those people who have experienced an NDE report all elements. (A measure of the depth or intensity of the experience, based on sixteen elements, has been developed by B. Greyson.)[6] Long's evidence for the afterlife is based on the number and consistency of reports and their description by NDE survivors as *real*.

There are several opportunities for further empirical research. Prospective studies (van Lommel, van Wees, et al., 2001)[7] have suggested that survivors of cardiac arrest who have had an NDE are more likely to have a positive life transformation than those who did not report an NDE. Since only 20 per cent report an NDE, how can we extend these benefits to the other 80 per cent? Both prospective studies and case-control studies might address these questions. The differences between NDE and non-NDE groups and the differences between those who have had a life transformation and those who have not are both worth studying.

Moody, James, and Long have provided intimate and descriptive discussions. However, for those who prefer an objective discussion of the NDE, I recommend the thoughtful and balanced article by Gideon Lichfield entitled "The Science of Near-Death Experiences" in the April 2015 issue of *The Atlantic*.[8]

Some Definitions

The Mind–Body Debate

The study of the NDE is at the centre of the mind–body debate between materialists and spiritualists. Materialists (which include most but not all medical doctors and researchers) hold that our mind and our thoughts are the products of our working brains, dependent upon the electrical and chemical actions of neural networks. When the brain dies, all the elements that constitute self—including consciousness, memory, mind, thoughts—are extinguished. Spiritualists believe we have an immaterial identity—you may call it a soul, life force, mind, consciousness—that is separate and distinct from our material bodies and can have a separate existence outside the body. The soul is the essential person—mind, thoughts, and emotions—and continues to exist in some other realm after death. In spiritualists' view, the NDE is evidence for a soul that can leave and re-enter the body.

Near Death and Clinical Death

Many experts on the NDE are vague about the difference between clinical death and near death. The commonly accepted medical definition of *death* is "irreversible cessation of all brain function." The key words are "irreversible" and "all"; and *irreversible* means exactly what it intends: there are no exceptions. *Reversible* or temporary cessation of brain function, or loss of consciousness, is common: sleep, anaesthesia, drug overdose, concussion, shock, cardiac arrest, and many other conditions. Reports of an NDE, without exception, are from those who have had a temporary and reversible alteration of consciousness. They are the experiences of the living, not of the dead. That is patently obvious, though seldom mentioned; the dead tell no tales. Medical science does not have a definition for *near death*.

The spiritualist definition of *death* is quite different; it is the moment when the soul (consciousness, spirit) leaves the body. No one has been able to determine the rules that govern this event, and some souls seem to be impatient, since they leave early, well before clinical death is established. The NDE cases are special, since they seem to involve a change of plan, where the soul separates prematurely and is then recalled, and the body restored to life.

All of this may be explicable by simply accepting that the storyteller has lost all sense of time. His perception of the event, his visions, may not coincide, either in timing or authenticity, with any specific event in the near-dying or recovery drama. All research in this field has started with the assumption that the images recounted by NDE survivors were experienced during the period of deepest unconsciousness. It is more likely that they occurred during awakening and are akin to flashbulb memories.

Those who report watching their own resuscitation are probably correct. Good CPR can maintain enough circulation to protect the brain, and I have seen patients in cardiac arrest recover consciousness during CPR. It is quite possible that some patients observe their own CPR, perhaps from a distorted angle.

Intuitive Logic

Is there a universal value of the NDE other than as a topic for sensational speculation? I have discussed the personal value as described by Brian, and I believe this is its main, if not the only, real value. Those who have had the experience enjoy a better understanding of life and death. But that describes only about 3 per cent of the population. Is there any benefit for the remainder of us?

Survivors and those who have studied the reports often claim that the NDE is proof of an afterlife. This is an intuitive proof, and unfortunately the evidence does not stand up to empirical scrutiny. In a world dominated by a scientific world view, we demand verifiable evidence, and it is not there.

However, despite our reservations, there are aspects to these reports that are very difficult to explain scientifically: their widespread consistency, lucidity, and aura of reality are striking. They are either evidence for an afterlife or a level of self-awareness impenetrable by any other means.

I HAVE SEEN A MIRACLE

We have all heard of medical miracles, but most of us have never seen one. We could, perhaps, agree that recovery from a life-threatening disease would qualify. True, but miracles are more than just fortuitous outcomes; they are rare events, otherwise they would not be miracles. They are unpredictable and defy medical explanation. Miraculous cures contradict the best medical opinion, leaving us amazed and perplexed.

Jacalyn Duffin, who held the Hannah Chair in History of Medicine at Queen's University for three decades, has made a study of medical miracles, especially those that have been accepted by the Catholic Church for canonization of saints. Her interest was piqued when early in her career she was asked to review a set of old blood and bone-marrow slides from a young woman with acute myeloblastic leukemia. She assumed the patient was long dead but was surprised to learn that she was in remission and doing well. Another surprise was that the request for an opinion was from the Vatican. They wanted to know if there was a scientific explanation for why this patient was still alive.[1] Dr. Duffin's evidence was crucial in the canonization of Saint Marie-Marguerite d'Youville (1701–1771), founder of the Grey Nuns of Montreal and the first native-born Canadian to be canonized. The patient whose slides she had examined had prayed to Marie-Marguerite.

Still, Dr. Duffin's opinion of medical miracles is very pragmatic: "These events were miracles for the people involved. The miracle, the thing of wonder, lay in the contemporary inability to explain the recovery."[2] They are cures that defy scientific explanation.

The following is a true story, and I will let Ian Dickson tell it in his own words.

In late October 2005, my wife, Donna, and I were in Florida for a holiday. While applying suntan lotion to my back, Donna noticed a mole that was discoloured and jagged in shape, and we agreed that I would have it examined upon our return to Winnipeg. In early December our family doctor removed the mole and it was sent to Toronto for pathology. A few weeks later I was heading home, singing along with the radio, as Christmas was only a few weeks away and retirement was being good to me. I stopped at the doctor's office to have him replace the bandage on my back. He asked me to sit down and told me the lab results were back and were not good; I had melanoma. I would need to see a dermatologist and oncologist as soon as possible. I went home in shock and told Donna the bad news.

We contacted a close family friend who was head of surgery at Health Sciences in Winnipeg and asked for advice regarding my next steps. He outlined the four stages of malignant melanoma and the treatment and prognosis for each stage, and asked that the lab results be sent to him for review. He called the next evening and advised that "we had a lot of work to do," as the melanoma was larger than four millimetres —an indicator of a likely poor prognosis. Through him, I was seen by both a surgeon and an oncologist very quickly, and my first surgery was done on January 23, 2006. I was able to avoid skin grafting in the area, but the sentinel nodes under my right arm were black—a sign, the surgeon said, was clearly cancer. A second surgery took place a few months later to remove the lymph nodes from that arm, six of which were involved with cancer.

Treatment of malignant melanoma involved interferon—a booster of my natural immune system. The side effects were that of a very bad flu, as interferon mimics the body's immune reaction. One month of IV treatment was followed by a proposed year of self-injections three times per week. I was advised not to make any big decisions during that year and that the effects of interferon may be reduced after finishing the IV treatment. I was also told that I might be giving up a good year for a bad one, given the seriousness of my diagnosis.

The flu-like effects did not subside after four months, and I spent most of the time sleeping and unable to enjoy much of anything. My oncologist had told me that I was in charge of my treatment and if I decided to stop at any time, my decision would be respected by the staff at Cancer Care.

In August of that year, Donna and I had a "come-to-Jesus" meeting and agreed that the additional year that I might get was not worth continuing the interferon, as quality of life was more important than quantity. As promised, the doctors respected my decision to stop treatment, and I was told that, based on statistics of melanoma, I would probably have about one year to live. This led to my identifying some short-term goals, such as playing the bagpipes again at the Grey Cup in November in Winnipeg and joining one of our sons for Christmas—and what a good Christmas it was!

My life returned to normal as I gained weight, returned to my workouts at the Reh-Fit Centre, and again enjoyed various activities with friends and family. I went to Cancer Care every three months for check-ups, then every six months until 2015, when the doctors and I agreed that I could finally stop these visits. The only residual effect of the interferon treatment is that I still have occasional difficulty articulating words and phrases. And my experience has made me appreciate my wonderful family, friends, and a medical system that helps one through such difficult times. I am especially grateful to my son, who gave me a diary at Christmas 2005 with the notation, "Dad, I thought you might want to write down your journey experiences as you move through this challenge of your life." I wrote in the diary until 2011, and I am still moving in 2017.

There are several flavours of miraculous experience. One is the dramatic escape, the unexpected survival, from something like a tsunami or an airplane crash. Such events are rare, but they do not violate natural or physical laws and therefore contribute nothing to our understanding of miracles. The majority of the miracles that have qualified as evidence for canonization were miraculous cures, and I believe Ian's recovery fits that mould, though I would be very surprised if he were on the Vatican's list.

The medical term for a miraculous cure is *spontaneous remission*, rare for cancer of this type.[3] There is no way to predict who will and who will not have a spontaneous remission. Some remissions last a few weeks; some, a few months. However, after fourteen years, do we still call it a *spontaneous remission*, a *miracle cure*, or something else?

We could follow social convention, call it *good luck*, and express our compliments in jovial banter. A hearty "congratulations, old boy, you are certainly a lucky devil" gives luck the credence of an active principle, even a personal quality. Good luck is applauded when it delivers, but it is too capricious. When we speak of luck in this way, we are fully aware that it simply covers up our ignorance of the real cause. Would you trust your life to luck? Not a chance! Luck is not a medical explanation for either good or bad outcomes.

Modern patients do not count on luck; they prefer a proactive approach. They are more informed and ask better questions, and they are more involved in their choices of treatment. In particular, they are willing to examine alternate treatments, especially those that empower them with more control over their lives. Some physicians complain that these patients are too demanding, but in the end we must (and do) acknowledge that it's their cancers we're treating.

Ian and Donna recognized after four months of medication-induced misery that they had lost control of their lives. For Ian, continuing treatment offered only the certainty of feeling terrible and the uncertainty of living longer. The decision to stop treatment was an expression of his autonomy; he acted as a modern patient should. Their description of the decision as a "come-to-Jesus" meeting indicates that they had not abandoned hope. It was a plea, not for a cure but for at least temporary respite from suffering.

The number of quotes about hope that have survived the ages attests to its central role in coping with personal tragedy. "Where there's life there's hope," attributed to Theocritus (c 270 BC), is still commonly heard. Sometimes the plea is desperate: Sir

Thomas More (1478–1535) before his execution declared, "A drowning man clutches at straws." Pragmatists, too, have their advice: "Hope for the best and prepare for the worst" (Thomas Norton and Thomas Sackville, sixteenth century). A quote more pertinent to our topic, however, is attributed to Dr. Martin Luther King Jr.: "We must accept finite disappointment, but never lose infinite hope." When medical treatment can offer no hope, we must look elsewhere. But where? Should we "clutch at straws" or seek "infinite hope"?

Our ancestors, who were less skeptical and more spiritual, did not find this a perplexing problem; they prayed with "infinite hope" and for divine intervention. Miracles were the evidence of God's love for humankind and demonstrated that nature was subservient to a higher authority. They were a reminder that randomness did not rule unchallenged. God's bounty was available to all; one need only pray with sincerity and accept God's will with faith.

Hope is no less important in today's secular world. When faced with life-threatening illness, we all start with the hope that medical treatment will be effective. However, when the disease is beyond treatment and medicine has nothing more to offer, hopes change. Some people accept their fate with grace and equanimity, hoping for peace, and some people may find comfort in prayer, in "infinite hope." Some persistently hope for a miracle cure and, "clutching at straws," pursue alternative treatments. And others, with resignation, simply trust to luck. If testimonial evidence carries any weight, every option has its share of success.

Cancer patients know that there is a small probability of spontaneous remission. Their faint hope for a cure is never completely extinguished. There are many ways to sustain that hope, and the choices are not mutually exclusive. A miracle bestowed by chance is indistinguishable from a miracle received by divine intervention. Ian and Donna did not question the source; they are content to enjoy the benefits. Whether you believe in luck or prayer or a magic herb, Jacalyn Duffin's conclusion still holds: "These events were miracles for the people involved."[4]

THERAPEUTIC PRAYER:
HAROLD'S STORY

This is a very personal account of one man's struggle with disease: a disease that was life-threatening, mutilating, prolonged, and painful. He not only survived but has also recovered his former good humour, confidence, and optimism. In this story he describes his mental suffering and his depression before he found solace in prayer. Harold's faith sustained him, and his confidence that his prayers were answered was the key to his recovery.

I chose to write about Harold's experience for several reasons. I knew that he was articulate and insightful, and could help us, as sympathetic spectators, share his experience and better understand both the physical and mental agony of life-threatening disease. This is his story in his words.

Harold's Story

My hip pain began in March 1995. I didn't suspect that it was just the first sign of a life-changing crisis that would challenge me both physically and spiritually. My profession as a physician had prepared me to deal with others as they faced serious illness, but I found that dealing with my own illness was much more difficult.

First, I will recount the story of my illness, and then I will describe the ways in which my faith supported me. The diagnosis of primary cancer of the pelvic bone (osteosarcoma) was made three months after the onset of my hip pain. My treatment was chemotherapy for six months and then massive surgery: an internal hemi-pelvectomy with an allograph (transplant) and a total hip replacement. In lay terms, this is the removal of half the pelvis and replacing it with a cadaver pelvis and an artificial hip. Limb-salvaging surgery was rare at that time and had been available for only about fifteen years in Canada. Prior to this, amputation or palliative care were the only options. In Canada this surgery was done only in Toronto, and only twenty-five people had had this operation in the previous ten years.

My chemotherapy was a horrible experience. I was nauseated, vomited frequently, and had two intravenous pumps beeping day and night. For seventy-two hours, I was unable to eat and was too weak to do anything. To stop the vomiting I took medications that scrambled my brain. I couldn't concentrate, and I was emotionally labile, sitting and brooding for hours. It felt like "hell on earth," and I was totally dependent, especially on my wife, Carolyn.

In November 1995, after six chemo treatments, I went to Toronto for surgery. The operation lasted ten hours, and I received seventeen units of blood. After six weeks in bed I started to ambulate but only with the assistance of three physiotherapists. My post-operative recovery was slow and delayed by many complications. First, my new hip dislocated. Then, just when I was ready to go home, a CT scan of my chest showed a tumour, so I underwent a lung operation (thoracotomy). Fortunately, the lesions were benign. Next, I developed an extremely high fever due to a deep-vein thrombosis, or blood clot, in my leg and a serious infection in my hip. I was placed on antibiotics and told to pray. I was slated to have my leg and pelvis removed in five days. Fortunately, my fever subsided with antibiotics, the amputation was cancelled, and, finally, on March 13, 1996, I was able to go home, four and a half months after my admission to hospital. When I left Toronto I had lost eighteen kilograms, could sit for only short periods, and could walk only short distances with crutches. I flew on a stretcher from Toronto to Winnipeg, but when we got home I finally felt my recovery was beginning. Carolyn and I had dinner with our family, and it was our first night in bed together in more than four months!

Now my weight is back to normal; my strength and energy have returned. I can now walk two kilometres with arm crutches, rarely nap during the day, swim frequently, read, and concentrate well. I have minimal pain and can socialize normally.

My leg was almost completely separated from my body during surgery and now has once again become mine. Initially, it felt foreign to me because some nerves were cut and others stretched. All my muscles and tendons were severed from my pelvis. Many have reattached to my new pelvis, and I now function at about 50 per cent of normal with crutches. Angels truly have protected my leg.

The pain associated with the medical aspects of my illness was difficult, but the mental distress was much worse. I spent many hours worrying about my illness and contemplating death. I was losing hope. The loss of hope inevitably creates a feeling of futility, our self-image drops, and our sense of worth is lost. We often forget, in this lost and fallen state, how important God is in our lives, but, fortunately, my spiritual reserves began to sustain me. When I was going through my deepest valleys of despair, I would turn to the Bible, and I found four scripture passages that helped me. They were Psalm 91, Psalm 103, Luke 11, and Romans 8. God would speak to me, and a "peace beyond understanding" (Philippians 4:7) would flow through me. God has promised us that any trial can be endured with His help. He helped Carolyn and me during the darkest moments, even when hope appeared to vanish.

I was not alone. Many friends counselled me during this time; others prayed for me in their churches, prayer cells, and personal prayers. These efforts of support were tremendously encouraging, but, ultimately, I was alone with my thoughts and found my solace in scripture.

Psalm 91

The key thought in Psalm 91 for me was that we are secure if we trust in God: "He who dwells in the shelter of the most high will *rest* in the shadow of the almighty" (Psalm 91:1). This security is not dependent on us or our circumstances: all personal disasters or crises are covered by the umbrella of security, which only God can give. There is, of course, a personal responsibility if we want this shelter. It is ours only if we are willing to follow God. If we choose not to dwell in God's shelter, we cannot expect to share in His promises.

As I read the passages in Psalm 91, my hope returned. I was reassured that I was secure even in my difficult circumstances. In my darkest hours my spirit soared. These promises were not just an abstract statement but also a real and powerful force for me. And, if you put your trust in Him, God will be your security even as He was for me.

Psalm 103 (A Psalm of David)

Psalm 103 is a psalm of praise and thanksgiving. After reading Psalm 91, how could I not be filled with praise? I was no longer focused on myself but was moved to praise God. What a change in emotions I experienced, from the depths of self-pity to the height of being in the presence of God himself. I could join David in singing praise in my heart: *"Praise the Lord, O My soul"* (Psalm 103:1).

David praises the Lord with his entire innermost being, an act that is especially meaningful to someone who is physically disabled; when we do as David does, our innermost being is intact, whole, and independent of our physical body.

Luke 11 and Romans 8

In Luke 11 and Romans 8 we see our relationship to God as our provider in all circumstances. I frequently cried out to God for relief of my emotional suffering and physical pain. When I felt that my problems were insurmountable, I would turn to the promises found in Luke: "Ask and it will be given to you, seek and you will find, knock and the door will be opened to you—for everyone who asks receives, he who seeks finds and to him who knocks, the door will be opened" (Luke 11:9-13). I did not pray that I would be healed. If we pray selfishly and the answer we receive is not what we expect, we blame ourselves for not having enough faith and God for not listening. Our responsibility is to pray in the will of God, which is clear if we read His word: He wishes us to love the Lord our God with all our hearts and minds and souls and to love our neighbours as ourselves.

My prayers during my illness were directed instead at the promises given to me in scripture: to give me peace under all circumstances. The psalmist reassures us by saying, "I am with you always, I will not tempt you beyond your ability to withstand it, you are my child and you will be with me in eternity" (Psalm 73:23). My prayers were answered with peace, patience, and self-control.

Many times I would pray, "Dear God, you have promised me the Holy Spirit. Allow Him to work in me and give me the fruit as promised," and a feeling of peace and joy would overwhelm me. The veil of fear and despondence left. This did not necessarily mean that I would be healed or restored to normality. This was not the important thing. I was not concerned about whether I would live or die but rather about how I would live until I died. Now my physical, emotional, and psychological states are much healthier, but I still pray that the Holy Spirit will be with me.

Romans 8 contains a letter in which Paul deals with the lifestyle of a person living with the Spirit. He discusses hope for the future. In times of stress and mental anguish, the whole concept of a continuing hope is often lost. At my lowest, I felt life was hopeless, and I knew that my thoughts had to be directed away from my misery and toward a bright and glorious future.

When we don't know what to pray for or how to pray, the Holy Spirit Himself intercedes for us, as does Christ Jesus, sitting at the right hand of God. We are in the hands of the Holy Trinity, who are all concerned for us and our welfare. This thought spoke to my heart and instilled in me a sense of perfect peace!

Since my return home, I have had twenty wonderful years of recovery with increasing strength and return to normality. When I have concerns I always return to the passages from Psalms, Luke, and Romans for comfort.

THE HEALING POWER

OF PRAYER

Harold's story is not about surviving the physical ravages of disease; it is about mental and emotional survival. It is a story that should be read in full and sympathetically, because only someone who has walked the road of severe illness can fully appreciate the emotional as well as the physical pain involved. Harold describes some of this pain, but he focuses more on the positive aspects, on the comfort and hope that he drew from his family and his Christian faith. His is a story about hope, love, and faith—and the healing power of prayer.

Modern scientific medicine has made such dramatic progress in treating and even eliminating disease that we tend to see treatment solely in terms of physical interventions: drugs, surgery, radiation, manipulation. The science of medicine dominates the field today, but the art of medicine is still important. Though the art is difficult to describe, and even more difficult to acquire, it embraces the subjective aspects of illness and the use of mental, emotional, and spiritual methods in healing. But being subjective does not put these factors beyond the scope of science. I approached this as a medical scientist and looked for empirical evidence for benefits. I found much more than I had expected.

First, a word of caution: please do not confuse the use of the word *spiritual* in this context with spiritual healing cults. The world is awash with such cults; just Google "spiritual healer" and you will be flooded.[1] Most cults claim to manipulate some sort of concealed spiritual energy or energy field, and a few are simply cover-ups. One recent promoter, as reported by Rachel Mendelson in the *Toronto Star* (February 21, 2015), conned his followers by promising that they would find a winning lottery ticket in a hard-boiled egg.[2]

Harold and I use the term *spiritual* not as a substance or force to be manipulated but rather as a personal conviction that there is a being, greater than us, who loves us and asks only for our love in return. Harold never expected to be healed by prayer; he prayed only for the strength to endure his illness.

Prayer can be offered for the benefit of others or for one's self. The first—prayers said by an individual or group for the benefit of others—is called *intercessory prayer*. The second—prayer for one's self—is *petitionary prayer*. Harold was the beneficiary of both. His church community prayed for him, and he prayed for himself. His often-anguished personal prayers are recounted in his story.

Intercessory prayer has been studied empirically by several groups, largely because it lends itself to the rigidly controlled studies necessary to ensure scientific validity. Leanne Roberts has authored three reviews in the *Cochrane Database of Systematic Reviews* that summarized by meta-analysis the randomized control trials (RCTs) published up to that date.[3] (Now, this is a heavy dose of academic shoptalk, so let me clarify the terminology. *The Cochrane Database of Systematic Reviews* is the repository for evidence-based medicine. A *Cochrane* review aims to summarize all the scientifically valid literature that has been published on a selected topic, and the RCTs are the gold standard for medical research. They are designed to measure the effect of one treatment, and only one, on a target outcome and are carefully edited and scientifically vetted. *Meta-analysis* is a statistical technique for combining the results of several studies.)

In their latest review (published in 2009), Roberts and her colleagues combined ten RCTs by meta-analysis (including 7,646 patients). You might be surprised to learn that there have been that many (ten) scientifically valid studies of this subject. And you might not be very surprised to learn that the results were equivocal. What does this mean, exactly? Well, some of the studies showed beneficial results of prayer and some did not, but the combined analysis did not reveal a statistically significant benefit.

Does this mean that there is no value whatsoever to intercessory prayer? No, only that the medical benefits are equivocal. The main, and perhaps the intended, benefit may be to the prayer group itself. Group prayer fosters group cohesion, common purpose, and shared values, and it reinforces faith. It enfolds the object of the prayer into the nurturing bosom of the community and reinforces group identity for all. Group benefit and individual benefit are difficult to separate.

Petitionary prayer has not been as well studied. In large part this is because it is so subjective and private. Since belief in the efficacy of the prayer is essential to the effect, it is difficult to conceive a study design where subjects could be randomly assigned to treatment (prayer) groups and non-treatment (no prayer) groups. However, there is a huge literature on religion and health outcomes, and most studies have used a general classification of religion/spirituality (R/S) to cover all aspects of belief, ritual, and prayer. The specific contribution of petitionary prayer is hidden in the whole. Two major reviews were published in 2015 with meta-analysis of literally hundreds of studies.[4] Both concluded that there was a positive benefit of R/S on several measures of patients' physical and functional well-being, including their symptoms and mental health. One of the striking benefits, reported by several studies, was increased tolerance to pain.

It is also interesting to note that there is a trend in the recent palliative-care and oncology literature to separate spirituality from religion. Medical providers are appropriating spirituality and relocating it into the biomedical and psychosocial fields of research. Spirituality is being reshaped to encompass considerations of the self and relationships while shedding the dependency on religious beliefs. A brief quotation from a recent review may give you a flavour of this change: "A 'spirit to spirit' framework for spiritual caregiving respects individual personhood."[5] How does this translate into better care for the sick and elderly? We await illumination.

The published evidence indicates that the benefits of prayer are mainly for subjective outcomes and coping behaviours, not for the physical aspects of the disease. Please note that, in all the literature documenting the benefits of prayer, there are no scientifically valid studies that demonstrate prayer to be an effective alternative to medical treatment. The main reason that prayer is held in disdain by scientists and medical doctors is the exaggerated claims made by some (Christian Science being foremost among them) that prayer can replace medical treatment. There is no credible evidence whatsoever for these claims. Prayer can be complementary to medical treatment, but it is not a substitute. If you read Harold's story in this collection, you will see that replacing medical treatment with prayer never occurred to him, not even when his treatment was causing him more distress than was his disease.

The benefits of prayer may be attributed to a phenomenon that has been well known since the dawn of medicine, called the *placebo effect*. Placebos are used as a sham treatment in most clinical studies; researchers recognize that a placebo-treated control group is necessary to separate the expectation bias from the treatment effect. There is also new interest in placebos in their own right as therapeutic tools. This has recently been noted in the popular literature by a feature article in the *National Geographic* and in the academic literature by the *Cochrane Reviews* and the *New England Journal of Medicine*.[6]

These reviews (again by mega-analysis) compared placebo-treated groups with no-treatment groups. The reviewers concluded that placebo treatment had a significant benefit when the outcomes were subjective and patient-reported, and especially for pain and nausea.

The placebo effect functions as a natural defence mechanism, and placebos act both by psychological mechanisms (perception and expectancy effects) and by triggering the release of endogenous hormones in the brain (endorphins and cannabinoids). The magnitude of the effects is still uncertain, but it is estimated that 7 per cent to 35 per cent of the number treated will have a beneficial response. Prayer, if it were offered with sincerity, could also be considered a placebo and may activate the same mechanisms. We await confirmation from appropriately designed studies.

Spiritual needs are traditionally met within a religious framework, and Harold's story describes how he found spiritual comfort in prayer and scripture, within his Christian faith. His faith in the power of prayer is confirmed by a vast literature, both lay and academic. Scientific studies as well as individual reports confirm that prayer, when offered with conviction, improves patients' well-being. Since most patients do not discuss their religious practices with their doctors, the medical profession's indifference to prayer is understandable. This is the business of hospital chaplains, but doctors rarely speak to them, either.

Prayer is relegated to the fringes of health care: it is private and secretive. It is recommended only as a last resort for those whom scientific medicine has abandoned. If prayer were offered as part of the treatment plan, would patients feel better, recover faster, and use less fentanyl? This is a challenge that our modern patients-first policy-makers might consider.

Harold and I were medical-school classmates and have been friends for more than fifty years. We share the same medical education and the same scientific view of medicine and disease. Harold is also deeply and sincerely religious, as his story shows. What we see clearly in his story, and others of similar genre, is that his religious and his medical responses to his illness were never in conflict. There is never a suggestion that his medical treatment was compromised by his religion or that his religion was threatened by medical science. His spiritual needs and medical needs were in different domains and required different therapy. Medicine and prayer were not just compatible: they were complementary. Those who claim that science has conquered religion, or that religion denigrates science, have a very shallow understanding of both. Harold's story shows that science and religion are not at odds; rather, they serve different needs towards the same end.

Prayer is a bridge that links the physical and spiritual domains of healing. Is there a scientific explanation for the efficacy of prayer? Not yet! While we can formulate and test hypotheses for the medical effects of prayer, the spiritual domain is opaque to our methods of investigation. I will, therefore, confine my speculation to the medical actions of prayer. The spiritual benefits I will leave to others to discuss.

I suggested earlier that we might consider the medical benefits of prayer in the same category as the placebo effect. This hypothesis might also be expanded to include other mind-altering exercises—yoga and meditation—which share common features. All aim for a mental state of enhanced self-awareness with increased receptiveness to the inner aspects of our minds while withdrawing from sensory and worldly distractions.

Consciousness and *self-awareness* are two important concepts in understanding how the human mind works. *Consciousness* describes a state of attentiveness that distinguishes between wakefulness and sleep, between normal alertness and the pathological states of coma, somnolence, and delirium. The simple clinical test of consciousness is to elicit an appropriate response to commands or to other sensory stimulation (a painful stimulus is one method). The essential neurological structure is the reticular activating system (RAS), an ascending system of interconnected neurons encircling the central core of the midbrain. The location of the RAS indicates its very early origin in the mammalian brain.

The mental state of being conscious implies, explicitly, that there must be some activity in the mind, some thought process (perhaps limited) that neuroscientists call *self-awareness*. There must, at least, be some recognition and processing of external stimuli (a painful stimulus). Self-awareness can exist only within the conscious state, and, in humans, self-awareness is considered an essential component of the conscious experience.

Self-awareness, in the cognitive sense, includes everything that we consciously experience in both our external and inner environments. This includes sensory awareness: the immediate experiences of our external environment through our senses. It also includes narrative awareness, in which we draw on memory and emotion centres to reflect on the past, present, and future. However, narrative awareness includes much more than just simple retrieval and reflection; its potential includes all of the higher abstract cognitive functions. We believe that it is the capacity for narrative awareness that distinguishes us from other species. Mind-altering exercises such as yoga act primarily on the narrative aspects of self-awareness.

Hans Lou[7] and his colleagues at Aarhus University in Denmark have spent several years developing what they call a *neuro-science of self-awareness*. They have used very sophisticated methods to identify neural correlates (specific brain areas) and neurotransmitters (messenger molecules) in different states of self-awareness. They hypothesize that the paralimbic network that serves self-awareness also plays a crucial role in balancing and regulating the allocation of brain resources. Disruptions of this network occur in developmental disorders of self-awareness like autism, attention deficit hyperactivity disorder (ADHD), and schizophrenia. They have also observed that meditation exercises (they studied Yoga Nidra meditation) were associated with activation patterns in these same areas of the brain that modulate self-awareness. These studies suggest that yoga is a tool that can be used to alter states of self-awareness.

The variety of human experience, on a minute-to-minute time scale, suggests intuitively that we must possess a control mechanism for channelling brain resources. Although we are not usually conscious of this control mechanism, we can see it in action in everyday activities: a very different set of resources is required for playing hockey from those for playing chess, for example. Psychologists have called this controller *metacognition*, without defining the actual brain correlates for this function (that is, the brain regions or neurotransmitters that specifically serve this function). Hans Lou and his colleagues believe it is part of the neuroscience of self-awareness. Despite its lack of precise location, *metacognition* is a useful concept in

that it identifies a process that is working constantly throughout our waking hours. Although we are mostly unaware of it,
it is certainly at least to some extent under conscious control
(concentration), and there is good evidence from mind-altering
exercises such as yoga and meditation that it can be trained.

The mind-altering exercises listed have been used to serve
specific mental goals: yoga for relaxation, meditation for
insight, and prayer for spiritual grace. Studies to date suggest
that all of these exercises aim to modify some aspect of narrative self-awareness by means of focused concentration: that
is, by excluding extraneous activity in order to channel brain
resources towards a specific goal (meta-cognition). We thus
have a theoretical mechanism for the medical benefits of petitionary prayer. Prayer, like other mind-altering exercises, acts
as a concentrating force that focuses self-awareness on positive
and healing narratives. The result is the placebo effect, a combined psychological and physiological response.

COMMENTS ON "THE HEALING POWER OF PRAYER"

All the stories in this collection were originally posted to my blog, <www.arnoldtweed.com>, as discussion pieces. Some attracted considerable comment, comment that added to the stories' scope and meaning. "Therapeutic Prayer: Harold's Story" and "The Healing Power of Prayer" in particular attracted a number of thoughtful comments and questions, and I have included some from Mike Czuboka and Garth Kidd in this chapter. I have known Mike and Garth for many years. Though they are far apart on the spectrum of religious belief, they have similar concerns: How can we reconcile a traditional god with our modern scientific paradigm of cause and effect?

Both Harold Wiens and I believe that the questions being asked here are important and relevant. Our responses are not the expert opinions of theologians but are the observations of students of human nature who have observed and experienced the effects of prayer in the therapeutic setting.

Mike Czuboka: Why is "faith" necessary? Why does God not just come out directly and tell us what we need to know?

Arnold: Good questions, Mike, that have puzzled many. Our story is based on a concept of spiritual benefit that I believe Harold and I both subscribe to. I will copy Harold with this message for his opinion.

There are two answers to your first question. The first, the one that many find unsatisfactory, is that God acts in mysterious ways. This is our heritage from the story of Job, who was punished by God though he was a good man. It portrays God as capricious, and a capricious god is of little comfort in times of need.

The second and more satisfactory explanation is that God does not work alone; He works with us and through us, not for us. Through the Holy Spirit of the Trinity, He offers His healing grace, which is freely offered but has one important condition. The grace of God must be accepted by faith; only then can its benefits be experienced. Rejected or ignored, it is of no help. God's grace is recognized by the supplicant in various ways: feelings of oneness, peace, hope, and all-embracing love. These are personal and subjective feelings, but there are too many such reports to doubt the reality of the transformation for those who accept God's love.

This explanation leaves the atheist in a Catch-22 situation. Having no faith, the atheist cannot experience God's grace. And having no experience of God's grace, the atheist has no faith. This is a conundrum that has only a conjectural solution. How can one acquire faith? It is an affective state of consciousness, which means roughly that it is something we know or feel innately, with certainty, and without need for logical proof. Generally, it is part of our family and cultural heritage, but it could come through various other life experiences, for example, through revelation or exercises such as prayer and meditation. These aspects of faith have been discussed by more insightful writers on this topic, writers such as Thomas Merton and William James.

Fortunately, you don't have to reject logic to accept faith; you simply have to understand that parts of our psyche never did and never will run on logic. (Logic is a late addition, an evolutionary refinement, in human history.) Logic explains how the material world functions, but it is intuition that explains how the personal world functions. The vast majority of our important life decisions—like choosing a mate or a profession —are based not on logic but on intuition. All our fundamental concepts of self (e.g., who am I?), particularly our spiritual self, are intuitive. Knowing something intuitively is the same as insight freed from the restraints of conscious reasoning. Plato described intuition as "the innate ability of the human mind to comprehend the true nature of reality." It draws upon the resources of the mind, such as memories, past experiences, pattern recognition, emotions, imagery, spiritual longings, and, yes, revelations. Some of these are hidden in that mysterious part of the subconscious that Sigmund Freud called the *id*. If empirical evidence and logical argument were the only paths to "truth," then faith must be rejected. But, if you listen to your intuition, you can have faith without offending your logic.

This is a rather long explanation, Mike, but I hope it explains why I was compelled to write this story. For a much more scholarly discussion, I refer you to Thomas Merton, *The Seven-Storey Mountain*,[1] and William James, *The Varieties of Religious Experience*.[2]

Harold: I would like to address your second question, Mike. Why does God not just come out directly and tell us what we need to know? I am not a theologian, but I have been a Christian since my youth. God has told us exactly what we need to know. My wife and I read through the Bible every two to three years. God has revealed his nature and what He demands of us clearly in the Old Testament. He also has revealed His triunal nature through the writers of the New Testament.

I challenge you to set aside all the philosophers and those who write about God and read what God says about Himself. At the least, read several books of wisdom: Proverbs and Ecclesiastes as well as Matthew, Mark, Luke, and John. If you have not had your questions answered, I would love to meet you and discuss these concerns you have.

Mike: I have read the Bible, but I find it to be confusing and contradictory in many places. Even dedicated Biblical scholars can't always agree on what the Bible tells us. The Protestant Reformation took place because some Christians did not agree with the theology of the Roman Catholic Church. Christianity today is divided into many factions with different interpretations of the Bible. And what about the billions of people, living and deceased, who have never heard of Christ? What about the radical Muslims who march to a different drummer and who will kill Christians if they do not convert? Why did Christians burn so-called heretics at the stake? Why did God not intervene? If God created us, why are we imperfect? That's a question I pose to Muslims as well as Christians. Does God answer prayers? He has not answered all of mine. Some good things have happened, but others have not. About six million Jews died in the Holocaust, even though many of them, I am sure, prayed desperately while being gassed, shot, and burned to death. Why did God not answer their prayers? How many Albert Einsteins did the Germans kill?

Arnold: These are all legitimate and penetrating questions, Mike, but theological rather than medical. I will simply offer you some of the assumptions I started with when I began this enquiry into the medical effects of prayer. Please note that I don't speak for Harold; he may disagree completely.

First, I read the Bible, both Old and New Testament, as literature. Certainly, there is a great deal of wisdom in both, but it is wisdom written by men (largely, if not exclusively, by men and not by women) and reflects the issues of their times. For example, the revival of Lazarus can be understood as a symbolic event, meant to convey an image of control over life and death.

Second, I view the institutions of religion, not just the Catholic Church but also all other forms of organized religion, as institutions founded by men (again) for the purposes of men. The only institution that I can trace back to Jesus is that of ministry. Therefore, when we look, for instance, at the celibacy of priests, or birth control, we can view them as the dogma of an institution, not a natural law. Similarly, we can view the crusades as products of the ambitions of men, not God. And so on!

As far as I can determine from my study of prayer as an aid to healing, the benefits are freely offered but received only by those who request them in faith and humility. I don't know what happens to the others. Perhaps they have other sources of spiritual succour that provide for their needs. In the current age our Christian god is often asked to provide spiritual comfort for those suffering illness, bereavement, or other personal tragedies. In Biblical times He was often reported to actively intervene in the affairs of the world, but there is little evidence for that now. The material aspects of the world have been left in the hands of the evolutionists and physicists. Any claims for his active intervention in world affairs—for example, the reassurances offered by George W. Bush and Tony Blair that He was on their side in the destruction of Iraq—should be met with serious skepticism. As a physician I see the purpose of God as exemplified by the ministry of Jesus, primarily as a healer and teacher.

Mike, I apologize for this feeble response to your questions. It is as close as I can come to a scientific explanation of God's works. William James pointed out, more than 100 years ago, that you could know God only by His actions. Our observations as medical scientists are limited to the actions in individual lives, such as Harold's. If we have not ourselves experienced these benefits, then our knowledge of God must be gleaned from the case reports of those who have. Case reports are accepted as scientific evidence if they are compelling, if what they describe is well outside the range of usual experience. Listen to the stories. Many of them are compelling!

Garth Kidd: I, too, have been trying to reconcile science and Christianity, not just for medical students but for everybody (including Christian spiritual leaders in particular). I believe science and Christianity to be joined at the hip.

I try to emphasize that Biblical writing and science writing have to be read in fundamentally different ways. Much, if not all, of the Bible is allegory, metaphor, and poetry, and is meant to be told as stories for people who were largely illiterate. Science writing is meant to be read literally, at least until physicists get to the point of describing electromagnetic radiation. Is it a wave or is it a stream of particles called *photons*? Come on . . . it can't be both!!! If it can, then you're using the word *wave* and the word *particle* metaphorically.

Hans Kung (a Swiss Catholic priest and president of the Foundation for the Global Ethic) gave a talk in London entitled "Science and the Problem of God." I had seen notice of his talk and happened to publish an article in the *London Free Press* one morning a few days later; Kung gave his talk that evening. As my late wife, Edna, and I were listening to his talk, she leaned over and said, "People will think you saw an advance copy of his talk. He is saying in theological language what you were saying in scientific language." Kung and I were saying essentially the same thing. There is no problem. You just have to read the script the way it was meant to be read.

As a result of my article in the *London Free Press*, I was invited to a ministers' breakfast next morning, where I had the opportunity to have a lengthy discussion with Kung. When we parted, he asked me to contact him if I were ever to find myself in Tubingen. Several years later, while enjoying a study leave at the Vant Hoff Institute in Amsterdam, I was giving a paper on magnetic resonance spectroscopy in the physics department at Tubingen for a physics friend whom I had met at an international meeting. I asked him if he knew Kung and explained the connection. He phoned Kung, and the two of us were invited to lunch. After lunch, Kung asked me if I would give a talk to his graduate students, entitled "Science and the Problem of God."

It was the only time in my career I gave a scientific talk and a religious talk within the same week.

Arnold: I enjoyed reading your comments, Garth. The analogy between theology and physics is insightful.

The law of gravity certainly is a human theory that describes the attraction between two material bodies. Newton's universal law of gravitation states that the attractive force is proportional to the product of the masses and inversely proportional to the square of the distance between the bodies. But this is just a mathematical expression of what we observe, and it does not explain the nature of *attraction* or *force*. Einstein's general relativity theory describes gravity not as a force but as a curvature of space-time. This exceeds my level of comprehension. I can experience gravity as a proprioceptive sensation, a sensation that I am pressed towards the ground, but not as a space-time warp. I have a similar problem with God; I can see His actions in stories such as that of Harold Wiens, but I can't picture God. Conceptual visualizations of gravity and God are equally mysterious to me.

William James stated more than 100 years ago that we can know God only by his actions. In that sense God and gravity are metaphorically similar; we know both only by their actions. The difference is that the action of gravity is universal, consistent, and predictable. The actions of God are not.

The post-Enlightenment scientific revolution has conditioned us to expect consistency and predictability, at least in the material world. Therein lies, I believe, the current general mistrust of religion.

The challenge for those who posit an important role for religion in the modern world is to demonstrate a consistent, reliable benefit. Fear of hellfire and damnation won't cut it. Neither will the concept of a capricious God who must be constantly propitiated. The challenge is to demonstrate the benefits of religious belief (or actions of God, if you prefer) during our mortal existence.

MALADIES OF AGING,
ENDURING MEMORIES

THE AGING BRAIN

What's your name? This is a question usually asked of a stranger, one of the first phrases you learn in studying a new language. Asked of a new acquaintance, it indicates interest and a desire to know him better. Asked of a child, it suggests that you respect the child as a person, as an equal. But when asked of someone you have known for fifty years, someone you have worked with, harvested with, played cards with, and chatted with almost every day of your life, it has an entirely different significance. It is a sign that the questioner's memory is failing, yet he still recognizes that something is familiar. Asking the question reveals that there is a struggle for recognition, that the other's face triggers old memories—someone he once knew—but the crucial item of identity, the name, is gone.

This is the most tragic stage of Alzheimer's disease: when the sufferer is losing contact with the essential parts of his past and realizes what is happening. He tries to preserve his shrinking world by filling in the missing pieces but immediately loses them. This was Roy in 1972, on his last visit to his old home, where he had been born, gone to school, and farmed for fifty years. It was where he had known everyone in the community since they had played together as children. But now he couldn't recall the name of an old neighbour.

We were going back for the annual picnic, Roy's last, though we didn't dwell on that. On the drive out, Roy and I had a long talk; that is—he talked, and I listened. For some time he had tried to deny his memory loss, but now it was time to face reality. He knew his memory was failing, and he was afraid. How could he carry on everyday activities, cope with finances, and enjoy his family if his memory were gone? How do you manage when your past is lost?

Roy was my father-in-law. He was small, wiry, and quick—quick both in movement and wit. He did chin-ups with one arm, not just one or two, but thirty, in a minute. A farmer who had survived the dirty thirties, he was by necessity an inventor. When he needed a new implement, he made it. One wet year when the rains delayed harvest, he built a swath turner so that the swath would be exposed, dry quicker, and be ready to combine sooner. He had a name for every animal on the farm and called each by name. When an issue of conduct arose, he invented a cautionary metaphor; he discouraged gluttony, for example, especially when new vegetables were so enticing in the spring, by citing the tragic case of "the girl north of Crandall" who ate so much that she burst. And Roy was a good neighbour; when a neighbour needed help, Roy was there.

By this time, his final visit to his old community, he knew that these parts of his life were slipping away. His hesitancy and uncertainty revealed a frightened soul struggling to recognize the shadows of his fading world. Fortunately, he didn't realize that even those shadows would soon disappear.

Alzheimer's is the most tragic disease that afflicts our aging population. It robs its victims of their past and of the memories that sustain them in old age. Without memory and recollections there can be no sense of identity, no concept of self. Without a past there is no future. Sufferers of Alzheimer's are eventually restricted to the immediate present, to the sensations of the moment and their gratification. Hunger is sated by eating; thirst, by drinking; itching, by scratching. Even the sensory present becomes narrower and narrower. Eventually, eating and defecation become the only activities that give satisfaction and, since all other sensory input has no meaning, sleep consumes the remainder of the day.

Is Alzheimer's the inevitable price to be paid for a long life? Not necessarily, but certainly the risk increases after age sixty-five and doubles roughly every five years thereafter. About 25 per cent to 35 per cent of those who live beyond eighty will eventually be affected with some type of dementia (see Figure 1).

Figure 1 PREVALENCE OF DEMENTIA BY POPULATION AGE

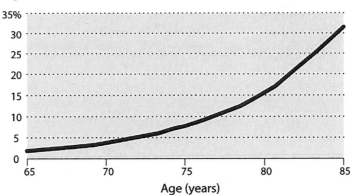

Graphics by Dean Tweed; data from the Alzheimer's Society of Canada.

Since women live longer than men, women with dementia will outnumber men with dementia by 2:1.

Alzheimer's is the most common of the age-related degenerative brain diseases that we collectively call the *dementias* (Parkinson's, Huntington's, and vascular dementia are others). The dementias impair cognitive function by specific pathological processes and are different from the biological changes of aging, the changes that we call *senescence*. *Senescence* describes the normal aging process, whereas dementias have pathological causes. There may be little difference in appearance between the senile and the demented, but the distinction is important.

Senescence affects all organs of the body, the brain included. But we all age differently, and cognitive decline varies greatly from one person to another. A partial explanation for this variability and a reason for optimism is that the brain at all ages retains a remarkable adaptive ability called *plasticity*, in which some functions can shift from an overworked part to a healthier area and even from one side to the other. Plasticity will help some of us reach old age with virtually no sign of cognitive deterioration.

But senescence is selective in another way, in that some cognitive functions are more susceptible than others. Memory is the first casualty, but to make things more complicated, memory loss, too, is selective; working memory and episodic memory are the first affected.

Working memory is defined as one's ability to retain a set of information (in short-term memory) and use it to plan, organize, and execute tasks. When working memory slows down, complicated tasks take longer and are done less efficiently. This may be hard to detect unless the ability is deliberately challenged—for example, by playing chess or bridge. Often, our major frustration will be in keeping a set of new information intact. This could be evident in everyday experiences. For example, Roy would want something that was in his tool shed but along the way would stop to putter in the garden, and when he arrived at the tool shed, he had completely forgotten why he was there. Sometimes the same happens to me!

Episodic memory is the recall of life experiences, the personal events of your life that are linked to specific times and places—the important bits and pieces of life stretching back to childhood. Senescence impairs the processes of forming (encoding), storing, and retrieving episodic memories; old, ingrained memories are better preserved, though retrieving them may take longer. You may remember your first day at school but not what you had for breakfast this morning, or whether anyone visited you yesterday (and if so, who was it?), or where you put your keys. Of practical importance, episodic memory is the fundamental skill for independent living.

Working memory and episodic memory are major components of a type of cognitive function that has been called *fluid intelligence*. The concepts of *fluid intelligence* and *crystallized intelligence* were introduced by Dr. Raymond Cattell,[1] who was at the University of Illinois in the 1940s. *Fluid intelligence* is the ability to process new and novel information, to find creative solutions to problems, to "think on your feet." Although fluid intelligence slows down with aging, other types of memory—factual (semantic) and procedural memories—are well preserved. These are what Cattell called *crystallized intelligence*: our generalized, encyclopedic memory bank. We remain proficient at tasks that use this type of memory—for example, doing crossword puzzles and, we hope, penning stories.

One special form of crystallized intelligence that is particularly well preserved is called *procedural memory*: walking, riding a bicycle, playing a musical instrument, reciting poetry. One very famous example is British musician Clive Wearing (born 1938), an accomplished chorus master who has complete amnesia due to a viral meningitis that destroyed critical parts of his brain (the hippocampus). His memory span is only a few seconds; his previous life is a blank slate. He lives in the ten seconds of the present but recognizes his wife (though does not remember her name), speaks fluently with an adequate vocabulary, and, when given a baton and an orchestra, can conduct flawlessly. His episodic memory is totally gone, but his procedural memory is well preserved.

We can't stop getting old, but can we slow the aging process? The Stanford Center on Longevity and the Max Planck Institute for Human Development in Berlin convened a conference of world experts in 2014 to examine the evidence. The main conclusion of the world's best minds in this field was remarkably prosaic: people should try to lead a physically active, intellectually challenged, and socially engaged life. How does that translate into everyday life? There is convincing evidence that a moderate level of physical activity, practised on a regular basis several days a week, is the most effective means of preserving both cardiovascular and cognitive function. Most studies conclude that a moderate level would be at least a half-hour of brisk walking a day. Riding a bicycle, swimming, or aqua-aerobics are good alternatives.

Being physically active is the easy part; the hard part is how to keep intellectually challenged after we retire. The key concept appears to be *productive engagement*, engagement in activities that require intense mental involvement—for example, taking a university course, learning a new language, or pursuing a new hobby.

Dr. Denise C. Park at the University of Texas at Dallas is a pioneer in these studies and has found that intellectually challenging activities improve the specific functions that deteriorate with aging: working memory and episodic memory.[2] On the other hand, the control groups in her studies—those assigned to *receptive (passive) engagement*—showed the effects of normal aging. Several other well-conducted experiments have now confirmed that the improvements in the productive engagement group are statistically significant.

Physical, mental, and social stimulation is not the elixir of youth, but it does slow the aging process. Old folks benefit from doing the same things young people do, perhaps even something as banal as video games. They probably benefit least from watching TV and listening to retired entertainers. There is mounting support for a holistic approach to aging, which emphasizes physical fitness, healthy eating, social stimulation, and cognitive exercises. Many of us can expect to stay physically active, mentally productive, and socially involved into our eighth decade. Old age may actually become a time for new adventures and new experiences.

That is the optimistic outlook for those who experience normal senescence. Alzheimer's and the other degenerative brain diseases are relentlessly progressive, though the pace varies and medication reduces the symptoms. Getting lost is often a critical turning point. Roy went for a walk one day, just for a block or two, and was found hours later almost two kilometres away and totally disoriented. This happened again and again, and finally required his admission to a chronic care facility. He adapted with equanimity to his new environment; the locked ward seemed to give him a sense of security.

Roy never saw his farm again, and even his home in the city quickly became unfamiliar territory. He was always anxious to get back to the security of the care home, and within a few months he was totally dependent.

The onset of Alzheimer's dementia is often slow, and there are no definitive tests. Early diagnosis is usually tentative and allows only a short window of opportunity for planning and preparation. At the time of his last visit to his hometown, Roy was in this window; he knew he was losing his grip on his world. This is the time for planning end-of-life care. Advance directives, if made while one is still mentally competent, will be honoured and can specify one's wishes to accept or forgo aggressive terminal care. Even when the disease has obliterated all semblance of self, we can still exert some personal autonomy over the quality of life remaining.

How did Roy fare in the home? He went through all the stages of dementia—dependency and the progressive shrinking of his world—and eventually, ten years later, succumbed to pneumonia. Our most famous Canadian physician, Sir William Osler, called pneumonia "the old man's friend." He was right; it is a gentle release from a life that has lost all meaning.

CLOCK AND CARRIAGE

My Grandfather's Clock

Ninety years without slumbering
His life seconds numbering
It stopped, short, never to go again
When the old man died . . .

   — Henry Clay Work (written 1876)

The Deacon's Masterpiece, or the Wonderful One-Hoss Shay

Have you heard of the wonderful one-hoss shay,
That was built in such a logical way
It ran a hundred years to a day . . .

Went to pieces all at once, and nothing first.

   — Oliver Wendell Holmes (written circa 1858)

Both these late-nineteenth-century poems express a universal desire for order and predictability. They presume a logical world designed by a logical creator, not the chaotic world we occupy. The grandfather's clock, figuratively, is an effigy of the Old Man himself. Its lifetime is exactly measured by the number of seconds it ticks, and it represents a harmonious world in which material and human destinies are intertwined. At the time the poem was written, it seemed completely logical that our lives should be programmed to a natural cycle, a fixed period of time, with an allotted number of seconds or heartbeats. When that allotment has expired, our time on earth is finished.

The wonderful one-hoss shay* expresses a similar longing for order. A logical creator would design things (and people) so that all the parts wore out at the same rate; at the end of their allotted lifespan, everything would stop at the same moment— "went to pieces all at once, and nothing first." Early critics have suggested that this poem was a satirical jest at the Puritans, but Holmes insisted that it was simply a comment on the absurdity of carrying practice to its theoretical logical conclusion, instead of relying on wise experience.

These poems are still popular and continue to intrigue us with their logical simplicity. They are allegories for the ideal human condition. If we must be mortal, then a logical creator would give us a fixed and predictable lifespan like that of the grandfather's clock—let us say, 100 years. And He would construct us like the wonderful one-hoss shay, each part equally durable and all expected to last for the same length of time.

I have known only one person who lived such a model life. My aunt Isabelle lived just a little short of 101 years. She died quietly in her bed one night with no obvious cause other than old age. My aunts of that generation, Isabelle and her sisters, were great talkers, and if there had been a measure of their allotted time, it would have been in words, not seconds. Isabelle had never suffered a major illness, and all her parts were functioning equally well. That is not quite correct; rather, all her parts were functioning equally poorly, as would be expected for her age. She was cheerfully alert when awake and enjoyed a family discussion—she still loved to talk, although the topics in which she showed interest were fewer than before. She got out of bed with assistance, ate her meals, and performed her toilette. The remainder of the day passed mainly in sleep. In other words she had all the functional capacity one would expect for her age. Her brain did not fail faster than her heart, or her liver faster than her kidneys. She had reached her allotted time, and no part of her was any better, or worse, than the rest.

*A one-horse shay (or one-hoss shay) is a light, horse-drawn carriage for one or two people. One-horse shays were very popular in America in the nineteenth century.

Very few of us will achieve that age and state of equipoise. Many will die before their allotted time, and many more will run down unevenly, sometimes one organ failing completely while others remain quite functional. Early Alzheimer's is a striking example; it's a disease in which every other body organ retains its natural vigour while the brain undergoes a relentless deterioration, destroying the essence of life. Whether from Alzheimer's or some other disease, most of us will die with the better part of our bodies still functioning quite well. We are not built like the wonderful one-hoss shay.

The logical ideal described by Oliver W. Holmes and by Henry Clay Work existed only in their imaginations. Unfortunately, we humans are the product of chaotic random selection, with no evident blueprint. Most of our basic cellular biology took form in the primitive dawn of life. Like primitive cells, we don't actually wear out; we just stop repairing ourselves. All our body organs, with some very important exceptions, are in a constant state of dying, repair, and replacement. Intuitively, we know that because our hair and nails continue to grow throughout our lives, our wounds heal, and, if we are male, our bellies grow while our biceps fade. Other organs behave in the same way: older cells are replaced regularly by younger ones. Biologists have studied the turnover time of cells in different tissues, so we could accurately calculate the approximate time for each organ to replace itself with new cells. In a book entitled *Cell Biology by the Numbers*, authors Ron Milo and Rob Phillips show that we have at least three types of tissue, each with a different cellular lifespan.[1] Some tissues, such as blood cells, replace themselves in a few days; others, such as bone and liver, in weeks to months; while a very small group must last our entire lifetime.

Each of these tissue types employs a different mode for regeneration. Most solid organs—the liver, for example—effect repair by a process called *mitosis,* in which mature cells duplicate their DNA and divide into two identical daughter cells. The daughter cells can do the same, for sixty to eighty cycles, before mitosis ceases and the cell line dies; only cancer cells can continue indefinitely. This limitation on normal cell division goes by the odd name of *apoptosis*, which simply means "programmed cell death." The nature of this cell-death program is a fascinating topic of research, and best evidence to date suggests that it has to do with cumulative damage to chromosomes, which eventually destroys their ability to divide.

But blood cells are very different from other cells. Mature blood cells don't divide but, rather, develop from progenitor cells— stem cells—which are located mainly in bone marrow. These cells are aptly named, since an embryonic stem cell, given the proper instructions, can form any of the more than 200 cell types in the body. Stem cells are the darlings of biology. At the moment, we don't know how to entice them to differentiate into specific tissues, but researchers are working on it. Unlike mitotic cells, stem cells are not limited in the number of offspring they can produce. Consequently, our blood system is programmed to last much longer than our livers or kidneys.

Some critically important tissues are not programmed for mitosis or apoptosis: for example, the brain and heart have no or little capacity for self-repair. The heart muscle is capable of mitosis at a very slow rate, but it is too slow to repair the damage of an acute myocardial infarction. Damage to the heart caused by infarction is replaced by scar tissue, not by healthy functioning muscle.

The brain has a unique method for growth and repair, different from all other organs. All brain growth occurs early in life, most in growth spurts from about seven months of gestation to puberty. Growth spurts produce a surplus of neurons and synaptic connections, all ready for action. Learning is rapid during this period, and synaptic connections are formed to establish countless arrays of working networks. The excess neurons and axons (that is, those that do not connect into working networks) are simply pruned away; they wither and are resorbed, a process called *remodelling*. This phase of growth and remodelling goes on for several years and serves a vital evolutionary purpose. The brain is most receptive and adaptable, and learns fastest, when we are young, but brain growth and repair cease by about twenty-five years of age. Synaptic connections can be strengthened after the age of twenty-five and new networks formed, but there is no regeneration of old neurons. The population of neurons at this age must last the entire lifespan.

What happens as we pass through middle and old age? Most brain processes—synaptic strengthening, pruning, and remodelling—go on throughout life, but at a slower rate. And, of course, after the growth spurts cease, there is no regenerative process for discarded neurons; they are not replaced. Therefore, shrinkage and atrophy of the cerebral cortices (brain senescence) is an inevitable consequence of aging. We are preprogrammed for senility.

Holmes and Work had a mechanical view of aging and were unaware of the most important part: senescence and age-related disease of the brain. Neither did they anticipate the potential of modern science. They imagined a logical world that at the time seemed rather whimsical and unrealistic. But medical science has become the new "logical creator" and may be able to craft what they could only imagine.

Medical science may one day—likely not in our generation —offer us the means to live longer, perhaps by extending the number of cell divisions before apoptosis or by training stem cells to replace failing organs. At first glance this seems an easy choice: of course, we want to live longer, but at what cost to ourselves and society? Will the price for longevity be prolonged brain senescence, which would make us burdens and not assets? The brain is the key. Until we can find a way to delay brain aging and stave off Alzheimer's disease, living longer would be a fool's fantasy.

Holmes and Work inadvertently provided the logical solutions to our quest for longevity. Although they saw their poems as amusing plays on logic, they offered very pragmatic examples in their analogies of the clock and the carriage. But how do we unlock the biological secrets so we can age like the clock and the carriage? My aunt Isabelle obviously had the answer, but she neglected to tell us. Perhaps when I last saw her, when she was 100 years of age, it had already slipped from her memory.

MIDDLE-EAST ADVENTURES,
SURVIVING SOLITUDE

THE LAST SPERM

An unusual mix of people gravitates to the Middle East. Most, like Glenyce and me, were there for the adventure, the cultural experience, and a tax-free income. Others, while undoubtedly sharing these noble motives, were there to put distance between themselves and the demons of their past. For the most part, those demons stayed behind, in the United States or the United Kingdom or Canada, but occasionally they surfaced in the most unexpected ways. Dwayne* was one whose demons were so much the fabric of his life that they followed him even to the remote Sultanate of Oman.

Back in the United States, Dwayne had been a rancher, a politician, and a biomedical technician, and each venture had ended with a misunderstanding, generally serious enough to warrant his repositioning. *Biomedical technician* was his job title in Oman, but the job was strictly a pastime. Dwayne organized camping trips, a softball league, desert treks, and backyard parties, and was everyone's friend and confidante. His past adventures became common knowledge, particularly his sexual exploits, which he was always happy to describe in appreciative detail.

His exaggerations may have been calculated to test the credulity of his listeners, but entertainment in Oman was in short supply and a good story was always welcome, particularly when the facts were impossible to corroborate. This is Dwayne's story, though a cautious reader should remember his fondness for a riveting tale. The plot itself belongs to an old genre, neither particularly original nor instructive, in which a deceitful woman

*To avoid embarrassment to anyone, I have falsified all names. Details of Dwayne's previous life are based solely on his accounts, and he had a reputation for embellishing his stories. My involvement was as an observer, not an active participant. However, I have heard the story independently from both principals at different times and am confident in the essential details.

leads a good man astray. Dwayne's penchant for intrigue and dissembling made him extremely easy to lead.

The story begins like a Harlequin romance. Dwayne, temporarily employed as an outrider in the chuckwagon races at the Austin rodeo, met a wild Texan woman and was immediately besotted. She was attractive, seductive, flirtatious, and volatile. They were soon a couple, and life was never dull; it was, according to Dwayne, an ever-changing kaleidoscope of new and exhilarating experiences. There was only one complication: sex was definitely in, but children were out. Her aversion to pregnancy was so intense that she insisted that Dwayne, in order to continue his unshielded pleasure, must have a vasectomy. Dwayne, eager to please and averse to the prospect of abstinence, agreed and arranged a surgical appointment for the earliest available date, a matter of a few weeks.

Dwayne was delighted by his new woman's sensuality but not entirely blind to her roaming instinct. A very little bit of sober reflection convinced him that the prudent course would be to anticipate other liaisons and possible future progeny. He began, therefore, to make regular deposits to a sperm bank with the resolve to create a sufficient reserve to adequately meet any future needs. Dwayne's exaggerated self-assessment of his future prospects necessitated a rather generous reserve, and he set to with enthusiasm. He had only a few short weeks and so took a firm grip on his new project and soon got into a regular rhythm. Weekly deposits soon became daily; the daily deposits mounted and were kept chilled in the refrigerator in a pint jar on the shelf behind the milk, labelled *Preserves* so they would not be confused with the whipping cream. His Texan woman, not nearly as committed to the venture as was he, did lend him a hand occasionally but soon tired of the exercise.

Despite his best efforts, Dwayne had difficulty satisfying the appetites of both his sperm bank and his woman, and her interest soon waned. While he was still struggling to fill his pint jar, she was seeking gratification elsewhere, and she left him while he was recuperating from his vasectomy. Dwayne was left with future progeny in cold storage and ready for safe sex but deprived of an outlet.

This did not last long. A rather serious misunderstanding with his employer regarding allocation of certain cash transactions led Dwayne to take a short-term job in the Philippines, and there he met Angela. She was stunning: just as gorgeous and sexy as the recently departed Texan but cut from a different cloth. Temperamentally, she was the complete opposite of the Texan woman: intelligent, sensible, and focused. And she knew exactly what she wanted: marriage, American citizenship, and children, in that order. The first two steps were easily accomplished, but after several months of valiant effort, the third was still wanting. Dwayne had neglected to tell her about his vasectomy. Although medical miracles do happen occasionally, miraculous reversal of a vasectomy has not yet been reported. When he eventually recalled all the details and was able to reassure her that artificial insemination was an adjunct, not a substitute, for natural sex, all went smoothly, and within nine months Angela delivered a healthy and robust male child whom they named Kevin.

I met them about a year later in Oman, where we both worked at the Sultan Qaboos University Hospital. In those days expatriates formed a tightly knit community and there were few secrets. In any case Dwayne did not have secrets: he was the pre-cyberspace equivalent of the Internet; everything he did was in the public domain. It wasn't long before Angela's maternal urges took control again, and we were all aware that Dwayne was under increasing pressure. But now the situation was very different from before: they lived in an isolated kingdom of the Middle East, and the sperm bank was in Austin, Texas. It was also nearing July, both the middle of summer and the beginning of Ramadan,* the Muslim holy month of prayer and fasting.

*My description of Ramadan is based on personal experience, having lived for many years in the Middle East. It is a month when subservience to Allah's commands takes precedence over all earthly matters. Work is considered an earthly matter.

But Dwayne, ever resourceful, had a solution. He sent a message to the custodians of the sperm bank with very specific and detailed instructions. They were to ship his sperm in a thermos—packed in dry ice and well insulated in a secure container—directly to him in Oman by DHL, an international courier. He was a bit concerned about how to label the package so it wouldn't be identified as a biological product and delayed for inspection, so he instructed that it be clearly labelled *Reproductive Aids*. The courier assured him it would be delivered within three working days.

Dwayne was at the DHL office in Muscat promptly on the third day . . . and the fourth and the fifth. Finally, a tracer on the package revealed that it had arrived on the last day of Shaban, the month preceding Ramadan, and it had been delivered to customs. This was routine; every item from international flights went through the customs shed, generally only for perfunctory approval before it was released. Only alcohol, pork, and pornography were confiscated. Perhaps they questioned reproductive aids as a legitimate import, but there had been no notification to that effect.

In order to appreciate the remainder of this story, you should have a short briefing on Ramadan. Ramadan lasts for exactly a lunar month. No Muslim shall eat or drink during the hours when the sun is visible. Practically, when Ramadam falls in July and the days are very long and hot, it is sensible to sleep for most of the day and eat, drink, socialize, and pray during the hours of darkness. The heavenly credits thus accrued are the same as if one had diligently worked all day.

Dwayne immediately started twice-daily visits to the customs office but, even if he could locate anyone awake, was always met with the same laconic response: "Nothing like that has come to our attention." His package had disappeared, had fallen below the threshold of attention, did not interest them, and did not merit the effort of a search through the mounting backlog of parcels overloading their shelves. Perhaps it was only three paces away, but to Dwayne it might have been on another planet. Dwayne's meticulous precautions had been his undoing; reproductive aids did not stir any sense of urgency in this bunch.

Good Muslims had no need for aids for reproduction; they managed quite well, thank you. In any case there was no hurry; sex was prohibited during Ramadan, and there would be plenty of time for such frivolity after fasting and prayer were done. And that was exactly the case: the package was not discovered until after both Ramadan and the subsequent post-Ramadan celebration, the Eid al Fitr, were over. After his precious thermos had sat for thirty-plus days on a shelf in the customs shed at forty-five degrees Centigrade, there was not a motile sperm in the lot. Several weeks of dedicated effort were pooled at the bottom of the flask in a rather putrid gel.

Dwayne was distressed, but Angela was inconsolable; her dreams were shattered. This was to be the supreme test of Dwayne's ingenuity. The next best thing to one's own sperm would be sperm from a donor who had demonstrated his potency—a proven producer. However, in a small and tightly knit community like ours, this could not be done surreptitiously. It must, in Dwayne's inimical fashion, be done publicly. His solution was to make it a sort of public contest.

Each day at noon the male employees of the hospital gathered for lunch in the hospital cafeteria. This was a daily ceremony, including not just lunch but also important discussions of work issues and next week's camping trip. Dwayne brought his wife to the cafeteria, unannounced, though the plan had been leaked to some of us (those not in the running). The plan was simply that Angela would unobtrusively inspect the assembled male cohort of the community and choose one to be the donor. She was to choose discreetly; Dwayne would then conduct the negotiations privately.

She chose Phillipe, one of my colleagues. Phillipe was a vigorous, muscular, red-haired Belgian with a great love of adventure. He also had a wife (his second) and two children, one from each marriage. His wife, Rachelle, was a petite, volatile,

French-speaking woman who was so erratically eruptive that I suspected she had a mild case of Tourette's syndrome. I bore you with this detail only in order to show that Phillipe had had some experience with emotional women. He also had a sense of humour, and, although surprised by Dwayne's request, he inexplicably agreed to the terms. His only excuse could possibly have been that he thought it was all a great practical joke.

However, it did not take long for Phillipe to grasp the two realities that he should have considered earlier: first, that Angela desperately wanted a second child and was very serious; and, second, that this would not sit well with Rachelle. He began to squirm. Unfortunately for him, his first attempt to squirm out of the deal was badly scripted. He informed Dwayne that he was a practising Catholic (which we all knew) and his priest had warned him that masturbation by a married man was a sin. He would honour his agreement if they insisted but only if it could be done the natural way. From this point the story gets a little murky, but it seems that Angela agreed to this with some conditions, the details of which are too private and delicate to expose publicly, so I will remain silent about specifics. Needless to say, Phillipe had now dug himself into a very deep hole and would have to do some serious backfilling. As I mentioned earlier, this was a very small community, and rumours of this pact had already reached Rachelle. As a good Catholic Phillipe understood that forgiveness of sin first demanded a full confession.

I was not there to witness this act of contrition, but several rumours circulated. Some reported that Rachelle exhausted both the French and English languages for words meaning *bastard* or some equivalent endearing terms. They were also amazed that such a petite and well-bred woman was so adept with profanity.

The denouement followed quickly. Kevin remained an only child; Dwayne's contract was unexpectedly terminated; Phillipe left for another job. Life in the expat community settled down to the normal routine of parties and camp-outs. The case of the last sperm is now believed by some to be simply a fabrication by a few who had spent too much time in the desert sun. Others think it was a masterful practical joke. The story has been retold several times, and I have heard the intimate details, independently and spontaneously, from both principals. If it had been just a practical joke, who was the perpetrator and who was the victim? To date, no one has confessed.

OUR BATTLE
AGAINST DEHYDRATION

My years in the Middle East taught me some profound lessons. One in particular has stuck with me: life in the desert is a constant battle against dehydration. During the five years I worked in Saudi Arabia, this battle became a major part of our lifestyle. You might assume that a prestigious job and a comfortable villa in the diplomatic quarter of Riyadh might protect one from such discomforts, but that was not the case for us.

Strictly speaking, it was not dehydration that tormented us but rather our need for beverages other than water and coffee. It was the extreme difficulty in acquiring even a mediocre bottle of table wine that distressed us. We had a thirst that could be slaked only by alcoholic beverages, but in Saudi Arabia they were strictly forbidden. This was not the only aspect of our Western lifestyle that was restricted, but it was the ban on alcohol that caused us the most irritation.

This is a story about adaptation—not how we and the Saudis learned to live together but rather about how we learned to live apart. Our coping strategies would be better understood if you could experience Saudi society as we did, as insiders. But, since that is not possible, I will provide some background. It is difficult to appreciate the Saudi Arabia we knew without knowing some of its history, so that is where I will start. I could briefly summarize this part by saying that Saudi society is dominated by two forces—religion and the ruling, al-Saud, family—but how that came to be is an interesting story.

Intolerance is not ingrained in Islam; however, it is a distinguishing feature of one sect of strict Sunnis, the Wahhabis, whose ancestral home is the desert oasis of Diriyah, just on the outskirts of Riyadh. The growth of Wahhabism as a political force can be traced back to 1744, the year that two Arab tribal leaders, Muhammad ibn Saud, emir of Diriyah, and Muhammad ibn 'Abd al-Wahhab, forged an historic pact that fused their political and religious ambitions. Both came from desert tribes living in one of the most desolate areas of the world, the remote desert of the Arabian Peninsula called the Nejd. Their meagre livelihood depended mainly on dates and camels, but both Muhammad ibn Saud and 'Abd al-Wahhab had greater ambitions.

Ibn Saud was a young and capable tribal leader who aimed to unite the desert tribes under his leadership. Up until then, tribal hostilities were generally limited to camel raiding by hit-and-run bandits, but ibn Saud was more than just a camel raider. The historic unit of governance was the tribe, essentially an extended family. When several tribes lived in a town, such as Mecca or Medina, one tribe might dominate but seldom forced the complete submission of the others. Ibn Saud's vision was a huge departure from traditional Arab custom and it violated the traditional tribal framework. He needed a cause to justify his ambition.

Muhammad ibn 'Abd al-Wahhab was stern and uncompromising. He was an aggressive reformer who had a fundamentalist vision of Sunni religion that was totally unpalatable to the other tribes. As a result he had few followers and his life was threatened. Ibn Saud, recognizing opportunity, took the al-Wahhabs under his protection in his tribal home of Diriyah. They sealed their contract in the usual fashion, with a marriage between their families, and the political authority of the modern Saudi state was forged in these blood ties. Under the terms of the pact, the Saud family had political and military authority, and the Wahhabs maintained control of religion and education. Ibn Saud now had his "just cause"—religious reform—to conquer and convert neighbouring tribes into a religiously fundamentalist al-Saud empire. Although that empire has twice suffered a major reversal, it is the pact between ibn Saud and Muhammad 'Abd al-Wahhab that governs Saudi Arabia today.

Muhammad ibn 'Abd al-Wahhab was the founder of a fundamentalist Sunni religious sect now widely known as *Wahhabism*. In Saudi Arabia its fundamentalist doctrines are encoded in Sharia (religious) law, and conformity is enforced by a ragtag vice squad, the *muttawa* ("religious police"). During our time in the kingdom, Wahhabism served as a tool for political and social as well as religious conformity. Religious observances are public rituals: prayer five times a day and the annual pilgrimage to Mecca (Hajj). All aspects of public behaviour were closely watched and regulated—dress, interactions between men and women, newspapers and magazines, radio and TV—and there were ineffectual attempts to regulate the Internet. The governing family was closely identified with the religious authority, so religious and social conformity was easily extended to embrace political conformity. Since the ruling family also controlled all the critical resources, the oil wealth of the country, and the police and the military, their control over the institutions and populace of the country was almost absolute.

Many Islamic scholars have pointed out that much of Saudi *morality*—that is, the behaviour regulated by Sharia law and custom—is not corroborated by the Koran or hadiths. It does not have authoritative references in Islamic theology but is based on social and cultural roots that go back to tribal life in the desert, and to Muhammad 'Abd al-Wahhab. Because tribal unity and trust depended heavily on blood ties and proven kinship, it was particularly important that the procreative activities of their woman be tightly regulated, hence the position of women in Saudi society today. In sociological terms, this type of morality is more accurately called *social mores*, or *cultural morality*.

In considering the relationship between the cultures of the West and Saudi Arabia, particularly for Westerners working in the kingdom, it is fair to conclude that the gulf between our notions of acceptable conduct was too wide to bridge.

Because Saudi Arabia, like all the Gulf states, depended heavily on foreign workers, foreign influences on Saudi culture were a constant threat. There were two groups of foreign workers. The non-Westerners—those from India, Pakistan, the Philippines, and other third-world countries—comprised the vast majority of the workforce. They were the oil-field labourers, construction workers, gardeners, domestics—all the jobs that a Saudi would not do. Their status was essentially that of indentured servants, and some were treated like slaves. Most were Muslim, and they were controlled with a heavy hand; minor infractions were severely punished, and they were constantly harassed by the muttawa. How the muttawa treated these people did not much trouble the Saudi authorities.

Western professionals, mainly in engineering, business, and medicine, comprised a very small percentage of the total expatriate community. They were in an unusual and privileged position: badly needed, somewhat admired, and generally protected from the methods of control most favoured by the state. Because the Western lifestyle was widely, though discreetly, admired, the Westerners posed the greatest threat to Saudi culture and religious authority. So the Saudi solution was to isolate them in gated communities, called *compounds*, where they could carry on their own ways without being seen or heard.

With all this information available in advance, what would tempt a Westerner to accept a job in Saudi Arabia and to move there with chattels and family? Perhaps the promise of an exotic lifestyle was most attractive, though a tax-free income was also tempting. But, once there, we strove to make the best of it, as the following anecdote illustrates.

Our isolation in the compounds forced us into closer bonds, and our social life became much livelier than it had been back in Canada. Since our social culture and traditional Saudi culture were so incompatible, any social interaction between us was impossible. Their cultural taboos made the things we enjoyed unthinkable in their company—things as simple as enjoying a glass of wine with dinner and having women and men eating at the same table. We therefore tended to have large, sumptuous, and very boozy dinner parties that included only close friends from the expat community.

But, you might protest, "What you say cannot be true. Earlier you stated quite emphatically that alcohol was totally banned." You would be right. The importation and sale of alcohol were banned. And, as you might expect, there was a black market, which was very expensive. Western expats all understood that no public display of alcohol consumption or drunkenness would have been tolerated. A suitable period of familiarization with the Saudi jails and then deportation would be the expected consequences. But most Saudis, excluding perhaps a few religious fanatics, were happy to conclude that if it were not seen in the streets, if it were not blatant, it didn't happen. This was a culture in which privacy of the family and sanctity of the home were highly regarded. The al-Sauds had a long tradition of protecting their privacy, and that benefit was extended to the Western expat community, who were essential to the portrayal of Saudi Arabia as a modern state.

It might already have occurred to you that the solution to the dilemma was to ferment our own. The supermarket we favoured had a complete aisle devoted to imported unsweetened grape juice, mainly from South Africa and Jordan. It was a fairly straightforward matter to add some sugar and a pinch of yeast, insert an air trap to maintain an anaerobic environment, and let it sit for about two weeks. Most of our houses smelled a bit yeasty during the process of fermentation, but after three to four weeks, we would have a reasonable facsimile of wine, at least reasonable enough to satisfy a thirsty expatriate who hadn't tasted real wine for several months.

Our dinner parties tended to be lavish and served to compensate for all the hardships imposed by separation from home. The particular dinner I write about marked a special occasion, perhaps someone's birthday, or maybe just the end of the week. It was catered by an Indian woman with a reputation for excellent cuisine. Her husband, George, was her only assistant. The rest of the staff were our houseboys and drivers, whose reward was to dine on the leftovers. How did we prevent them from also sampling the wine? Monitoring was totally unnecessary!

All the staff, including the chef and George, were Muslims. They watched each other closely. If there had been only one staff member, we might have had a real fear that he or she would drain the heels of the bottles and become a problem. But with a group, there was absolutely no concern.

We were a party of eight, all Canadian and all medical people—a convivial lot who had shared this type of cultural therapy many times before. There were many compliments on the wine, which slaked the desert thirst only if consumed in sufficient quantity and with proper appreciation. It is not surprising that some time late in the evening we may have become a bit boisterous. But, hell, we were in our own sacrosanct space behind a ten-foot wall with two of our drivers on alert for intruders; we were not fearful of the authorities.

Late in the evening, after we had imbibed copiously, we were suddenly startled, not by intrusion from outside but distress from inside. George had been quiet all evening but was now slumped in a chair in the kitchen, sweating profusely, moaning, and clutching his chest. He was obviously having an acute myocardial infarction, a heart attack. We had been too involved in our celebration to notice that his discomfort had been increasing all evening, until the point when he could no longer conceal it. George had been previously well and had no history of angina or other heart problems. We immediately suspected that his heart attack was stress-induced and related in some way to the events of the evening.

One of our drivers whisked George off to hospital. We instructed him not to go to a government hospital but to go directly to the King Faisal Specialist Hospital, the premiere tertiary-care hospital in the kingdom, where a colleague was on emergency duty. If we, his employers of the evening, were responsible for his medical crisis, we would also ensure that he got the best care available.

In the morning, after all our guests had left and some tidying was in order, I counted sixteen empty bottles. Even for this group that was a remarkable achievement. Although we were all quite civilized, our behaviour must have appeared bizarre to our Muslim cooks and servants. This was a recurrent cultural abyss that was impossible to cross, and we could never fathom whether their superficial indifference covered astonishment or dismay.

Was our drinking so shocking that the stress triggered George's heart attack? Was it his guilt about being an accessory to sin? Or was he simply terrified that we would be discovered and he would land in a Saudi jail? In retrospect, I think that the latter cannot be totally discounted. Islamic law—that is, Sharia law—is harsh and uncompromising. If, by some fluke of circumstance, we had been discovered, the Muslims among us (that was everyone but the eight Westerners) would have been treated very harshly. Aiding and abetting such immorality would be considered as serious as was drunkenness itself, and their punishment would likely have included jail and flogging.

Awareness of the rigidity of Saudi culture and the harshness of Sharia law is certainly a sobering reality, but the question is: Should those be the sole guides to one's conduct? What is perceived as sinful in one culture may be perfectly acceptable in another. Can it be morally acceptable to drink alcohol in one culture (Canadian) and morally wrong to drink it when living within another cultural framework (Saudi Arabian)? This would imply that one should comply with the culture of the host country when living and working in that country, and it would leave one quite free to switch when travelling abroad or returning home. This is a dilemma that has troubled many expat workers but also troubles Saudi citizens who study or travel abroad. We often criticize Saudis who switch their cultural identity when they leave the kingdom but forget that we do the same. Resolving these questions of ethics and morality would seem to be a basic requirement for coping with life in Saudi Arabia. In truth, however, we gave it very little thought.

If we had been more perceptive, we might have discerned a moral message in this incident. Perhaps George's medical emergency was an omen meant for our instruction. Since there can be only one god for Muslims, Christians, and Jews, we can reasonably assume that God and Allah think alike. God's punishments are often puzzling; He sometimes punishes the innocent, as in the case of Job, in order to instruct the sinners. Was George's affliction meant as a warning to us to mend our ways, a gentle reminder from Allah that we were not completely beyond his jurisdiction? Certainly, the next morning we all had some regrets, and for several days our preferred drinks were water and coffee. But this was due to the after-effects of overindulgence, not moral misgivings. We suffered for our excesses but not enough to mend our ways. The lesson was too subtle. Like Moses, we could see the burning bush, but we did not recognize the angel of the Lord in the flame of fire (Exodus 3:2). We should not flagellate ourselves too severely; even the Apostles had difficulty at times understanding the parables of Jesus. If there had been a moral lesson in this incident, we missed it! The next week we continued our convivial ways with another dinner party and no less appreciation for the host's homemade wine.

How does one cope with a culture as inhospitable to Westerners as that of Saudi Arabia? Our understanding at that time was that it would have been foolish to risk ourselves, and particularly our servants (who were almost all Muslim), by publicly flaunting the Sharia law of the kingdom. We were also well aware that private and public morality served different masters. Achieving the secular needs of the kingdom required that some constraints be placed on the muttawa, the much-feared and much-despised religious police. What was done privately and discreetly was outside their sphere of authority. This applied to the Saudis as well as expats. Saudi culture is anchored by a profound respect for the sanctity of the home.

Our less-than-dry nights in the desert are now fifteen years in our past. We still enjoy dinner parties, but we now consume much less wine. It is true that one craves the forbidden fruit. Our friends from that time are still our friends, though they are now spread across several continents. Our houseboys and drivers all eluded the muttawa and have gone home to India to tell their stories of the orgies they attended.

Society is changing in the Middle East, but in what direction? I believe that their future lies with their women; more than half the students in their universities, including medical schools, are female. They are the hope for the nation. But will change be orderly and incremental or precipitous and bloody? Either seems possible. My wife and I have no desire to go back to watch it unfold, just as we have no desire to relive our battles against dehydration!

MISCHIEF-MAKERS,
PRIVATE AND PECULIAR

LABELLING

My wife and I perform a silly little ritual every morning, usually while we're still in bed with our first cup of coffee. We test each other, question and answer, on mundane matters, roughly the same list of questions each day, though for variety we mix the order. First, we cover the easy questions: name, date of birth, and address. But our real focus is on the tricky questions of day and date, month and year. Often we finish with some general-knowledge questions—for example, the names of the current and previous prime ministers. Why do we do this ridiculous exercise every day? In medical jargon it is called *orientation*; it is the basic test of mental competence.

If you have been in a hospital recently as a patient, you will have had an orientation check. It is done by the first—and usually most junior—nurse and, if you are over sixty, it will have been done thoroughly. Moreover, parts of the checklist will be repeated with each transfer to a new set of caregivers.

Nurses take this very seriously; it determines whether they treat you as a person or as an object. If you have given an incorrect answer to any question (date is the most troublesome), you will perhaps have noted that the nurse looked at you long and thoughtfully, then wrote something in your hospital chart. What she writes is a flag that will be clear to everyone who subsequently reads your file. It will determine where you lie on the scale between person and object. From that point onward the staff will be more condescending and will explain everything twice, and everything they do will be prefaced by the question, "Is that okay?" They will be extra careful that the seat belt on your wheelchair is secured and that the side rails of your bed are locked. You will be required to wear a hospital gown—open at the back and exposing your buttocks—and paper slippers. And any objection on your part will only confirm that you are indeed demented.

Now, to explain why Glenyce and I do this every morning: we are preparing for the unforeseen emergency, for the sudden chest pain, the fall, or the drunken driver who might throw us into the medical system with no opportunity to rehearse. If hospitalization is thrust upon us, we intend to be prepared.

This would not be an issue if it were a one-off—only an irritation for a single admission. But once that *demented* entry is in your file, it is never erased. From that day on, as long as your medical file exists, you will be treated accordingly. Your medications will be counted for you and you will be watched while you swallow your pills. You may find a tag with your name and hospital ward pinned to your gown. In the worst case, the *House of God* scenario, your diagnosis will become your identity—you will be referred to as "the demented old hernia on ward six." This is called *labelling*, and it is one of the most pernicious phenomena of medical recordkeeping. A label, once entered on your chart, is never changed or erased. It is part of your persona for the rest of your life.

Glenyce was recently almost caught in this trap, and perhaps this was the incentive for our present diligence. She was having vocal-cord surgery because of hoarseness and was being interrogated with the routine pre-surgical checklist. Those questions are exact and always in the same order: the patient is asked to name the type of surgery, the site, and whether it is to be on the right or left side. Now, this generally makes good sense since, in the past, the most common surgical error of misidentification was operation on the wrong side: amputation of the wrong leg, arthroscopy of the wrong knee, or excision of the wrong breast. However, when hoarseness is the issue, it is impossible for the patient to know which vocal cord is affected. When the critical question was asked for her vocal-cord surgery, Glenyce, not having prepared, had no ready answer. Knowing the consequences of a wrong answer, she almost panicked. The nurse, who was both very young and very serious, had begun her long, penetrating look, and her unease clearly mounted as the silence continued. How could she let this demented old lady, who couldn't even remember on which side her operation was to be, go on to the next station? The nurse was just about to write this in the chart when I prompted Glenyce by surreptitiously scratching the right side of my neck. She quickly got the clue and interjected the correct answer just in time. It was a close call!

But, surely, is this not just the paranoia of someone with a poor short-term memory? Unfortunately, the medical literature confirms that it is not. The ground-breaking research was done almost fifty years ago by David Rosenhan, an American psychologist and Stanford University professor who was skeptical about psychiatric diagnoses and the labels pinned on those with mental illness. He was the chief investigator of the famous Rosenhan experiments, and the results were published in *Science*, in an article entitled "On Being Sane in Insane Places."[1]

In the first part of the study, Rosenhan and seven completely sane associates—pseudo-patients—presented to different psychiatric hospitals with identical, factitious stories, claiming that they had auditory hallucinations. All were admitted, but from the time of admission they acted with perfect normality and did not report any further hallucinations or other symptoms. They were all labelled with a psychiatric diagnosis (mainly schizophrenia) and prescribed anti-psychotic drugs (which they flushed down the toilet). The average length of stay was nineteen (a range of seven to fifty-two) days, and they were discharged only after they had acknowledged both the diagnosis and their need for treatment. This happened despite the fact that they had acted perfectly normally from the moment of admission. Even their practice of questioning other patients and taking notes, part of their research mission, was cited as evidence of psychosis. The original diagnoses were never questioned or revised.

These results, as expected, offended the prestigious psychiatric hospitals, and one of the more prominent of these challenged Rosenhan to repeat the experiment, claiming its staff could identify his pseudo-patients. During the following weeks, 41 of 193 admissions to that hospital were identified by the staff as pseudo-patients—that is, as imposters. In fact, Rosenhan had sent none. He concluded, publicly, that psychiatrists were unable to distinguish the sane from the insane. The Rosenhan experiment showed that labelling is often a reflection of the expectations of the examiner rather than the state of the patient. And once a label is in your file, it is very difficult to remove.

Rosenhan was the first to identify labelling as a medical expediency, but it was Samuel Shem in *The House of God* who raised labelling to a literary art.[2] His *gomers, slurpers, LOLs,* and *LOMs* with *NAD* (nothing abnormal detected) have become ingrained in the cult language of "med speak." His is the extreme of labelling, a dehumanizing cult activity that was meant as black humour. Though these terms are out of favour today, others have replaced them; for example, a severely demented person may be called a *vegetable* (partly because the original medical description called this type of extreme dementia a *vegetative state*).

I am not opposed to all labelling. Some labelling is pejorative and annoying, and some is amusing, but some is essential.[3] There is neither space nor time here to discuss the broad spectrum of labelling, so I will limit myself to a short primer on how to avoid the pejorative labelling associated with aging.

Historically, there have been numerous metaphors for aging, some appealing but most not. Calling an older woman an *old gal* is a bit patronizing, but *old biddy, old crone,* and *old bag* are definitely insulting. An old man, on being called a *gaffer,* might not have grounds for umbrage, but *old goat, old geezer,* or just *granddad* may be intended to get his dander up. Overall, few of the labels our society has pinned on the aged are complimentary, and many are downright demeaning.

I hope that I, and you, my readers, have avoided the most damaging labels, but we must think of the future—the labels that we do not deserve. Since we are dealing with perception, not reality, perhaps we can subvert the process, cultivate our own labels. Do you have favourites? I do.

Why not cultivate a benign but plausible label that has personal wearability? Sport a bow tie, drive a 1994 Ford, eschew email. That would certainly earn you a label (probably *eccentric*). These are not my personal props, of course, but to reveal them would blow my cover. Mine work for me, and I don't mind being called absent-minded or even a little strange. Most of my friends already expect me to act a bit oddly and are not offended if I forget their names. Labelling of this sort can be used to your advantage, but beware, even if you are not the persona behind the label, you will soon begin to act the part. Choose carefully!

However, I still advise an orientation exercise every morning. Medical labels confer few benefits, and to be labelled *demented* is the least attractive. It is particularly galling if done by an exacting young nurse, fresh from training, and just because you couldn't remember the date.

A MINOR PROCEDURE

When I was an intern, I treated several patients who left lasting impressions—even scars—on my psyche. One was an autistic boy whose one delight in life was to push small stones up his urethra until it was obstructed. Usually the stones could be flushed out with a catheter and warm water, but in my nightmares I can still hear the clangs as they were expelled into the kidney basin. That experience, decidedly Freudian, has left me with a particular distaste for having anything inserted into my body orifices. It is more than distaste—it is visceral revulsion that is accompanied by cremaster muscle spasm. I'm sure everyone has similar sensitivities and phobias.

I am soon to have a trans-urethral resection of a bladder tumour, considered a minor surgical procedure, and in preparation for that, I will need to have another minor procedure, a saline enema. Sounds easy, but this is my first personal experience with either of the procedures. My medical experience does not count here; I am a novice patient. Even a simple enema, when I am to be the recipient, especially given my revulsion for having anything inserted into my personal body orifices, is much different from the abstract notion of *enema*. As a doctor I would simply leave an order on a hospital chart for a saline enema, and, I must admit, I have never actually given an enema to a patient. Nurses have always relieved me of that unpleasant chore.

My problem now was: How do I give myself an enema? One does not find instructions for self-administered enemas in prestigious medical journals, and it is too private a matter to be discussed in party banter. Practical directions are hard to find. Recognizing that performance under duress might compromise both the results and the environment, Glenyce and I decided that an enema drill would be in order. Don't confuse this with carpentry drills; we didn't intend to drill the enema into position. We have called it a *drill* in deference to my military service, though in this case we didn't aspire to true military precision and order. Our low expectations proved to be prescient, and the exercise was an invaluable experience in improvisation and persistence. It also led me to appreciate some of the misconceptions that I have been complicit in promoting during my years of medical practice.

Both those who manufacture enema equipment and those who prescribe enemas have a vested interest in promoting them as casual, routine, everyday—even pleasant—adjuncts to almost every probing or scoping of the lower body orifices. One of the reasons I chose anaesthesiology as a specialty was to avoid any but the most necessary contact with those parts of the anatomy. Now that my position has changed from that of net provider to net consumer of medical care, my concern—particularly for my own orifices—has been considerably sharpened.

The first point to note is that the instructions to "give" an enema conceal a complete misunderstanding of the dynamics. How to "receive" an enema is the more important and relevant consideration. This is just one of the euphemisms that mask the true nature of this and other "minor" procedures. I don't wish to bore my readers with unnecessary detail, but let me elaborate briefly on one aspect of the procedure.

Positioning is a crucial factor in the success (or failure) of the whole exercise. Recommended positions are described in the equipment package insert, along with hints of the consequences if these instructions are carelessly disregarded. "The recipient should be in a bathtub or on several layers of towels," directs one insert. After the choice of either the bathtub or towels is made, three positions are recommended: the fetal position, the knee-chest position, or the missionary position. Of course, with flexibility and imagination, many more are possible, but these three will suffice for the beginner. For the fetal position, one is advised to grasp each knee with the ipsilateral hand and pull the knees in a cephalad direction to make contact (or as close as possible) to the chest while lying in the lateral position. This, of course, totally eliminates any possibility of self-administration. We chose this for our first enema drill, and the recipient (the "enemee," me) positioned himself, possibly more in the interests of decorum than convenience, in a bathtub facing the giver (the "enemer"). This, of course, made it quite impossible for her to reach the assigned orifice without also entering the tub. In the resulting melee of arms, legs, and orifices, the contents of the bottle went down the drain (wrong orifice). This was the end of Drill #1.

For Drill #2 the enemee assumed the knee-chest position. For those unfamiliar with this position, I recommend that you spend a weekend watching porn movies. You will undoubtedly see several variations, and you can choose the one that best suits your purpose and preferences. This position is arguably better suited to the bathtub, though, again, access can be compromised. A position with the designated orifice in close approximation to the taps and shower head is not recommended. In our Drill #2 inadvertent contact with the cold-water tap by the enemer resulted in a reflex spasm by the enemee and a premature ejection of the fluid ($14.99 per bottle). Drill #2 was also written off as an expensive but useful learning experience.

For Drill #3 we tested the DIY missionary position (not intended to be an oxymoron). Having had two unsatisfactory experiences in the bathtub, we did this on the floor—on several towels, of course. The positioning here has some resemblance to the knee-chest position but in the supine rather than the prone position. There are two options for this position. One can grasp the knees with the ipsilateral hand and pull them cephalad, the traditional position for missionary sex. However, that manoeuvre tends to oppose the buttocks, and some experts recommend grasping the knees and pulling with the contralateral hand, which acts to separate the buttocks. This is the only feasible position for self-administration, if one ignores the previous advice concerning the hands. I should warn the prospective DIY buff that deft handling of the container is definitely a two-handed job, one hand to remove the cap and the other to steady the bottle, and the legs have to be left to their own devices. Clumsiness in any of these steps can result in external, rather than internal, application of the enema solution. Unfortunately, we also had to write off Drill #3. Since each trial was necessarily followed by a calming libation, this was starting to eat into the refreshments budget as well.

Fortunately for us and our budget, Drill #4 was successful. The enemee assumed the contralateral missionary position, and the enemer, on hands and knees, grasped the cap of the bottle in her teeth, rested her weight on one hand, and deftly inserted the nozzle with the other hand. Squeezing the bottle to an empty state with one hand was a challenge, but inspiration provided a solution. By raising herself to the kneeling position, she freed both hands to squeeze the bottle and at the same time was able to peer between the knees of the enemee and share his satisfaction as the bottle emptied. Mission complete!

The novice, however, should be aware of one more possible misunderstanding of the instructions. The recipient is advised to retain the enema solution for fifteen minutes before expelling the bowel contents. The written instructions offer no advice regarding activities during this time and leave the impression that "carry on as usual" is in order. Based on my experience, I advise that one spend that fifteen minutes in very close proximity to a suitable receptacle, preferably the toilet bowl. The expulsion can be both uncomfortably spontaneous and explosive.

There is a serious note to this nonsense. From a patient's perspective there is no such thing as a "minor" procedure. Even something as simple as an enema can be fraught with anxiety and frustration. My drills with the enema were not for pleasure but in serious preparation for a "minor" and "minimally invasive" surgical procedure. If I were starting again, I would expunge the term *minor procedure* from my medical vocabulary.

NOTES

Preface

1. For a definition of *djinn*, see *Islam Question and Answer*, <https://islamqa.info/en/26266>.
2. E. Becker, *The Denial of Death* (New York: Free Press Paperbacks, 1973).

Munchausen's Syndrome

1. R. Asher, "Munchausen's Syndrome," *The Lancet* 1, no. 6650 (1951): 339–41.
2. G. P. Yates and M. D. Feldman, "Factitious Disorder: A Systematic Review of 455 Cases in the Professional Literature," *General Hospital Psychiatry* 41 (2016): 20–28.

A Visit to the Doctor

1. *Black shit*, a black, tarry stool, indicates serious bleeding high in the gastrointestinal tract.
2. The guaiac fecal occult blood test is an older but simple test for occult (hidden) blood in the stool, blood that is not visible on the surface. Guaiac paper for the test is prepared from the wood resin of the guaiacum, a tropical tree commonly known as *lignum-vitae*. This tree has several medicinal uses, now only of historical interest.
3. S. Arya, "Parentheses," *Canadian Medical Association Journal* 190, no. 3 (2018): E82–E83.

In Memory of Garm

1. V. Morell, "From Wolf to Dog," *Scientific American* 313, no. 1 (2015): 60–67.

Three Jewish Daughters

1. For discussions of the stereotypical Jewish mother and the Jewish American princess daughter, see: E. Bazelon, "Never Mind, I'll Just Sit Here in the Dark: A Brief History of the Jewish Mother," 2007, <http://www.slate.com/articles/life/family/2007/06/never_mind_ill_just_sit_here_in_the_dark.html>; and J. Antler, *You Never Call! You Never Write! A History of the Jewish Mother* (New York: Oxford University Press, 2007). See also: I. Asimov, *Asimov's Guide to Shakespeare* (Garden City, NY: Doubleday, 1970).

Joe, We Need You!

1. Joe Doupe was born and educated in Winnipeg and graduated with his MD in 1934. His first interest was medical research, and he went to England for post-graduate studies with E. Arnold Carmichael at St. Bartholomew's Hospital in London. His early studies in autonomic control established his reputation as a promising medical scientist, but this phase of his career was interrupted by World War II, in which he served as a medical officer with the Royal Marine Corps.

   The end of World War II found him back in Canada and applying for a research position at the University of Manitoba Medical School. Dean Alvin T. Mathers was impressed by Joe's achievements, and, with funding help from Dr. Paul H. T. Thorlakson, co-founder of the Winnipeg Clinic, Joe was appointed the first director of the Department of Medical Research at the University of Manitoba and, in 1948, the head of the Department of Physiology, a position he held until his retirement due to ill health in 1966. Joe died from complications of his diabetes in 1966 and was survived by his wife, Nona, and three children.

   It is of historical interest that Joe's appointment was aided by the support of Dr. Charles Code (1910–1997), a Winnipeg contemporary who had also studied in the UK and later made his reputation at the Mayo Clinic as one of the pioneers of allergy research, clarifying the role of histamine in allergic reactions and in acid secretion by the stomach. Code is best known for helping solve the serious World War II problem of pilot blackout during high-G manoeuvres.

Joe is generally acknowledged as the most important intellectual influence on the modern University of Manitoba Medical School—now the Brady School of Medicine. Dr. Arnold Naimark, former dean of Medicine and president of the University, described his influence this way: "From him we learned that the independent mind is the guarantee of security of the scholar from the tyranny of transient fashions in medicine and permits reason to rise above passion" (Dedication address by Dr. Arnold Naimark).

2. M. Wente, "Why Campuses Are Ditching Free Speech," *Globe and Mail* (Toronto), March 20, 2017.

3. G. Lukianoff and J. Haidt, "The Coddling of the American Mind," *The Atlantic* (September 2015): 42–50.

4. S. Kedzior, "At Long Last, a Forum Where Trump Cannot Escape the Truth," *Globe and Mail* (Toronto), March 21, 2017.

5. E. Montpetit, "After Potter: Media Pool or Knowledge Institution?" *Globe and Mail* (Toronto), March 30, 2017.

6. A. Potter, "How a Snowstorm Exposed Quebec's Real Problem: Social Malaise," *Maclean's* (20 March 2017). https://www.macleans.ca/news/canada/how-a-snowstorm-exposed-quebecs-real-problem-social-malaise/.

The Absurdity of Life

1. For a summary of the life and work of Albert Camus, go to: <https://www.nobelprize.org/nobel_prizes/literature/laureates/1957>. His acceptance speech for his Nobel Prize for Literature in 1957 can be found at <https://www.nobelprize.org/prizes/literature/1957/camus/speech/>.

2. A. Camus, *The Myth of Sisyphus, and Other Essays* (New York: Knopf, 1955), 212.

A Beating Heart in a Warm Corpse

1. I have not disguised any names or details in this story. They are all part of the public record, either in newspaper articles or court records. Cpl. Junor's mother gave consent to harvest his kidneys for donation, but I never saw her again. Unfortunately, when researching this story, I was unable to locate any next of kin. Cpl. Juror is buried in the military section of the municipal cemetery in Estevan, Saskatchewan.

2. The Princess Patricia's Canadian Light Infantry (PPCLI) is one of Canada's most distinguished regiments. My father served with them in the First World War and was wounded during the heroic defence of Frezenberg (second Battle of Ypres) on May 8, 1915. My nephew by marriage, Lt. Gen Ray Crabbe, is a retired commanding officer of the regiment and led the Canadian contingent including members of the regiment during the peacekeeping operation in Bosnia.

3. Many of our ancestors had a morbid anxiety about the possibility of a premature diagnosis of death. They were afraid that the appearance of death might be an illusion and were reluctant to abandon the hope for spontaneous revival. It was a custom in some parts of sixteenth-century England to hang a small bell over new graves with a cord hanging down into the coffin, so that the not-quite-dead, awakening in the claustrophobic confines of the grave, could signal for help.

4. Brain death can now be diagnosed with certainty by cerebral angiography or radio nucleotide scanning, which measure intracranial blood flow. When the brain is lethally damaged by trauma, stroke, or tumour, it swells, and this swelling increases the pressure inside the skull, a closed space. When the intracranial pressure is equal to the systolic blood pressure, circulation of oxygenated blood to the brain ceases. These techniques can accurately confirm complete absence of perfusion of brain tissue at all levels. An organ with no blood flow is a dead organ and will soon enter the stage of biologic decomposition. Brain death is

now generally accepted as equivalent to death of the person, though the heart may continue to beat for some time and keep other major organs alive.

Suspended Animation

1. All the St. John's Cathedral schools are now permanently closed, but the St. John's School of Alberta, which closed in 2009, maintains an alumni office at the school site in Stony Plain, Alberta. Their website is <http://sjsa.ab.ca/>. The definitive history of the schools (*Today My Sail I Lift*) was edited by Mike Maunder, a former teacher. It can be purchased from the alumni office.

2. The story of Edward Milligan's miraculous recovery was widely covered in Canadian newspapers and published as a case report. See: G. Bristow, R. Smith, J. Lee, A. Auty, and W. A. Tweed, "Resuscitation from Cardiopulmonary Arrest during Accidental Hypothermia Due to Exhaustion and Exposure," *Canadian Medical Association Journal* 117, no. 3 (1977): 247–49. See also: "Clinically Dead, 16-Year-Old Keen to Get to School," *The Ottawa Citizen* (Ottawa), February 20, 1976, p. 12. <https://news.google.com/newspapers?nid=2194&dat=19760220&id=EWk1AAAAIBAJ&sjid=rOoFAAAAIBAJ&pg=1159,1917133&hl=en>.

Near-Death Experiences

1. E. Alexander, *Proof of Heaven: A Neurosurgeon's Journey into the Afterlife* (New York: Simon & Schuster, 2012).

2. *Flashbulb memory* was first described by Roger Brown and James Kulik, psychologists at Harvard University, in 1977 ("Flashbulb Memories," from <https://doi.org/10.1016/0010-0277(77)90018-X>). I quote from their original abstract: "The principal two determinants appear to be a high level of surprise, a high level of consequentiality, or perhaps emotional arousal." Obviously, this also describes the

NDE. The abstract of their paper can be found online at <http://www.sciencedirect.com/science/article/pii/001 002777790018X?via%3Dihub>. For the original reference in the medical literature, see: R. Brown and J. Kulik, "Flashbulb Memories," *Cognition* 5, no. 1 (1977): 73–99.

3.   R. A. Moody, *Life after Life* (New York: HarperOne, 2015), 174.

4.   W. James, *The Varieties of Religious Experience*. The Gifford Lectures, 1901–1902 (New York, London: Longmans Green & Co., 1902). This book and James's other writings are available for free download from the Gutenberg Project: <https://www.gutenberg.org/wiki/Main Page>.

5.   J. Long and P. Perry, *Evidence of the Afterlife: The Science of Near-Death Experiences*. The Near-Death Experience Research Foundation (New York: HarperOne, 2010).

6.   B. Greyson, "The Near-Death Experience Scale: Construction, Reliability, and Validity," *Journal of Nervous and Mental Diseases* 171, no. 6 (1983): 369–75.

7.   P. van Lommel, R. van Wees, and I. Elfferich, "Near-Death Experience in Survivors of Cardiac Arrest: A Prospective Study in the Netherlands," *The Lancet* 358, no. 9298 (2001): 2,039–45.

8.   G. Lichfield, "The Science of Near-Death Experiences," *The Atlantic* (April 2015). <https://www.theatlantic.com/magazine/archive/2015/04/the-science-of-near-death-experiences/386231/>.

I Have Seen a Miracle

1.   J. Duffin, *Medical Miracles: Doctors, Saints, and Healing in the Modern World* (Oxford, New York: Oxford University Press, 2009), 285. Jacalyn Duffin is now professor emeritus, retired Hannah Chair, in the History of Medicine, Queen's University.

2.   Duffin, *Medical Miracles*, 183–85.

3.   Survival with malignant melanoma depends on the stage of the tumour. The worst is Stage IV, in which the cancer has spread to tissues distant from the primary site; in

medical language, it has *metastasized*. At the time Ian was diagnosed, the outlook for Stage IV disease was very grim. He was given a generous estimate of about one year to live. The authority for statistics on cancer is the American Joint Committee on Cancer (AJCC), administered by the American College of Surgeons. The AJCC reviews all cancers, and there is a section identified as Melanoma Staging and Classification. This section updates their reports at regular intervals, and those reports can be found online. To review the latest information on staging and outcomes, Google AJCC Melanoma, or go to: <https://cancerstaging.org/CSE/Physician/Documents/Melanoma%202.2.18.pdf>.

4. Duffin, *Medical Miracles*, 183.

The Healing Power of Prayer

1. There is a host of spiritual healing cults, all with enticing promises. Spiritual healers and some so-called alternative providers claim to be able to manipulate an invisible energy field or spiritual energy by contact healing. Some are simply scams, as reported by the *Toronto Star* in 2015 (Rachel Mendelson, February 21, 2015, p. GT6), and none can produce any credible evidence to support their claims.

    Medical authorities distinguish non-conventional practices as *alternative* or *complementary*. As the names suggest, alternative practices are promoted as replacements for conventional medicine; complementary practices are used together with conventional medicine; and the combination of complementary and conventional treatment is sometimes called *integrative* medicine. For an expert medical perspective, see the statements of the National Institutes of Health (USA) and the Mayo Clinic (<https://nccih.nih.gov/health/integrative-health; <https://www.mayoclinic.org/healthy-lifestyle/consumer-health/in-depth/alternative-medicine/art-20045267>).

Prayer is lumped together with meditation, relaxation, and art therapies. Harold and I place prayer firmly in the complementary group; it is not an alternative to conventional treatment and certainly not to be confused with spiritual healing.

2. R. Mendelson, "Purported Spiritual Healers a Widespread Problem," *Toronto Star*, February 21, 2015.

3. L. Roberts, I. Ahmed, S. Hall, and A. Davison, "Intercessory Prayer for the Alleviation of Ill Health," *Cochrane Database of Systematic Reviews* 2 (2009): CD000368.

4. There have been literally hundreds of studies of the effects of religion/spirituality on health outcomes. Two meta-analyses of these studies were published in 2015. In these studies, petitionary prayer is not singled out, since it is so personal and private. Both studies were published in a credible scientific journal with a robust peer-review process. See: H. S. Jim et al., "Religion, Spirituality, and Physical Health in Cancer Patients: A Meta-Analysis," *Cancer* 121, no. 21 (January 2015): 3,760–68; and J. M. Salsman et al., "A Meta-Analytic Approach to Examining the Correlation between Religion/Spirituality and Mental Health in Cancer," *Cancer* 121, no. 21 (November 2015): 3,769–78.

5. Another meta-study indicates that palliative care researchers are co-opting spirituality and separating it from religious belief and practice. See: N. Edwards, N. Pang, V. Shiu, and C. Chan, "The Understanding of Spirituality and the Potential Role of Spiritual Care in End-of-Life and Palliative Care: A Meta-Study of Qualitative Research," *Palliative Medicine* 24, no. 8 (2010): 743–50. The quotation is from page 1 of the abstract.

6. The placebo effect has always been a part of medicine, though perhaps not always recognized. We have been aware of the placebo effect in medical research for over fifty years, since described by Henry K. Beecher, an anaesthesiologist. But, as Eric Vance has recently discussed in the *National Geographic*, the effects extend much beyond medical research.

Reviews in the *New England Journal of Medicine* and the *Cochrane Database* confirm our clinical impressions. Placebos have a significant benefit, particularly on patient-reported outcomes such as pain and nausea. See: H. K. Beecher et al., "The Effectiveness of Oral Analgesics . . . and the Problem of Placebo 'Reactors' and 'Non-reactors,'" *The Journal of Pharmacology and Therapeutics* 109, no. 4 (1955): 393–400; E. Vance, "Mind over Matter," *National Geographic* 230, no. 6 (2016): 30–55; A. Hróbjartsson and P. C. Gøtzsche, "Placebo Interventions for All Clinical Conditions," *Cochrane Database of Systematic Reviews* 1 (2010), <https://www.cochranelibrary.com/cdsr/doi/10.1002/14651858.CD003974.pub3/full>; and A. Hróbjartsson and P. Gøtzsche, "Is the Placebo Powerless?" *New England Journal of Medicine* 344, no. 21 (2001): 1,594–1,602.

7. Hans Lou is a former colleague and good friend. Some of his research work was done in our lab at the Health Sciences Centre in Winnipeg in the 1970s. His publications are too numerous to list here, but, for the interest of the scientifically curious, I will offer one. The rest are available from PubMed. See: H. C. Lou, T. W. Kjaer, L. Friberg, G. Wildschiodtz, S. Holm, and M. Nowak, "A 15O-H2O PET Study of Meditation and the Resting State of Normal Consciousness," *Human Brain Mapping* 7, no. 2 (1999): 98–105.

Comments on "The Healing Power of Prayer"

1. T. Merton, *The Seven-Storey Mountain* (New York: Harcourt Brace, 1998).

2. W. James, *The Varieties of Religious Experience: A Study in Human Nature* (New Hyde Park, NY: University Books, [1902] 1936).

The Aging Brain

1. R. B. Cattell, "Theory of Fluid and Crystallized Intelligence: A Critical Experiment," *Journal of Educational Psychology* 54, no. 1 (1963): 1–22.

2. See: D. C. Park and A. H. Gutchess, "Long-Term Memory and Aging," in *Cognitive Neuroscience of Aging*, ed. Roberto Cabeza (NY: Oxford University Press, 2005).

Clock and Carriage

1. Biology aficionados who are fascinated with all things numerical will enjoy this book. How long does it take to replicate half the cells in the liver? About a year. Half the white bood cells? About five days. See: R. Milo and R. Phillips, *Cell Biology by the Numbers* (New York: Garland Science, Taylor and Francis Group, 2015).

Labelling

1. D. Rosenhan, "On Being Sane in Insane Places," *Science* 179 (1973): 250–80.

2. S. Shem, *The House of God* (New York: Berkeley Books, 1978). Reissued by Penguin Publishing Group, 2010.

3. Some labelling is simply the result of mental laziness: our need to organize our world, to pigeonhole, to reduce the number of items in our working memory. It reduces the complexity of social interactions when we can lump people together under a label rather than treating them as individuals. But it also affects our sense of identity and behaviour and how we are perceived by others. For example, someone labelled as *sickly* is more likely to play the sick role, to believe she is sick, and to be seen by others as sick. The label sends a message to the patient (and family) and to society.

    Despite the occasional misuse of labelling, some medical labels serve an essential social need; one example is the labelling of perverted killers as *sexual psychopaths*.

Dr. Marnie Rice, who spent a medical career studying these offenders at the Pentetanguishene Hospital for the Criminally Insane in Ontario, concluded that *sexual psychopath* was a fixed and untreatable personality disorder, and attempts at treatment, especially group therapy, simply made psychopaths more adept at manipulation. Protection of society demands that this label be taken seriously and that sexual psychopaths be confined for life. Serial killers such as Paul Bernardo, Clifford Olson, and Robert Pickton must never be paroled. See: G. Tharras, M. E. Rice, V. L. Quinsy, and C. A. Cormier, *Violent Offenders: Appraising and Managing Risk* (Washington, DC: American Psychological Association, 2015), 236–37.